The third book of
Paint along with
NANCY KOMINSKY

Oil painting made easy

by Nancy Kominsky

COLLINS
Glasgow & London

Nancy Kominsky

Nancy Kominsky, a native Philadelphian, is a portrait painter, an international lecturer, teacher and author, who now lives in Rome, Italy. She studied at the Graphic Sketch Club, Philadephia, Pa. Cooper Union, New York City and under Theodore Lukits, well known portrait painter in California. She worked for three years doing painting and sculpturing on scaled dioramas for a Pennsylvania Museum.

In 1963, faced with the prospect of no income and at the urging of a friend, she opened her first Sunday Painters Art Studio in Burbank, California. She devised a unique 'anyone can paint' system of teaching which became instantly successful.

In 1966 she moved to Rome and opened the equally successful Sunday Painters of Rome, teaching personnel from all the embassies of the world how to paint. She has completed three highly acclaimed networked television series in Britain, of thirteen programmes each, called *Paint Along With Nancy*, and has written very successful accompanying books. Now there is a Nancy Kominsky television series in the United States based on this internationally famous, unique method of teaching people to paint.

She is the mother of two children who live in California.

For all the paintings in this book Nancy Kominsky has used Rowney Georgian Oil Colours which she has found to be the most suitable for her purposes. They are permanent and their consistency is incomparable for palette knife painting.

First published 1976
Published by William Collins Sons & Co. Ltd, Glasgow and London

Designed and edited by Youé and Spooner Ltd

Filmset by Tradespools Limited, Frome, Somerset
Printed in Great Britain
ISBN 0 00 411841 3

Contents

Introduction

When I started teaching, I discovered that along with the instinctive need for survival was man's instinctive need to express himself, to record his environment. This is not new. It began thousands of years ago with the cave dwellings of our ancestors.

That creative urge has not changed. It is still there in each and every one of us.

All through the years I have heard the same refrain from students and people from all walks of life, all over the world: 'I have always wanted to paint,' and that has included such well known people as Churchill, Eisenhower, and even Grandma Moses, who at seventy years old became famous for her primitive paintings.

It is evident that nearly everyone has a secret desire to paint, but they are often put off because they believe painting is a mysterious, involved process, which only a talented few can understand.

Therefore I decided to remove the mystique from painting (amid howls of protest from the experts) with the 'anyone can paint' approach, giving all those who wished an opportunity to enter this happy world and enjoy the pleasures of painting.

The method I have devised consists of three basic guidelines which will guarantee you, the absolute beginner, an acceptable painting on your very first attempt.

1. The preliminary drawing is done with the aid of grid lines applied with brush and umber wash. The drawing shows the correct placement of components, stroke directions and tonal values.

2. Colour formulas are given in exact amounts for the mixing of the three tonal values needed.

3. Paint is applied with a palette knife.

Finally, when you have mastered the basic skills of painting, you will be free to decide for yourself what 'ism' to adopt or create, and the conventional pictures used in the painting lessons in this book can be a launching pad into space of abstract, avant-garde art — the Picasso of today is not the Picasso of yesterday.

Now relax and enjoy yourself. Don't become frustrated and discouraged trying to become another Michelangelo or Van Gogh. Painting is exciting and fun and that's what it's all about.

Happy painting!

Painting materials

The following colours and other required painting materials, which are illustrated on page 9, can be purchased under the Nancy Kominsky label. However, you can buy them separately, if you wish, from most art material stockists.

No substitutions of colours should be made, otherwise your colour mixes will not turn out the same as those in this book.

PAINTS

Lemon Yellow
Yellow Ochre
Naples Yellow
Cadmium Yellow deep
Cadmium Orange
Vermilion (red)
Alizarin Crimson
Viridian (green)
French Ultramarine (blue)
Burnt Umber
Extra large tube of Zinc or Flake White

PALETTE KNIVES

Offset knife, for painting
Straight knife, for mixing colour (optional)

BRUSHES

1 large, flat hog brush, for umber wash
1 medium round brush, for drawing

OTHER MATERIALS

Easel — whatever available and sturdy. A table easel is very useful if you are short of space as, not only does it fold away, but the table on which you place it then provides a good surface on which to put all your painting supplies.

Turpentine, or white spirit if you do not like the smell of turpentine. (This is the medium for cleaning your brushes.)

Large square wooden palette or tear-off palette pad.

Single tin dipper for the medium of turpentine or white spirit.

Canvas or canvas boards, 36cm (14 in.) by 46cm (18 in.). If you do not want the expense of either of these, use hardboard which is adequate. Go to a timber yard and have a large piece cut into 36cm (14 in.) by 46cm (18 in.) sizes. Paint each piece with cheap white undercoat on either the rough or smooth side (depending on your preference) and leave to dry thoroughly before use.

Toilet tissue which is disposable and therefore more practical and cleaner than cloths.

Plastic litter bag.

Polythene or tin foil. Use either of these to cover your left-over paint on the palette, pop it in the fridge and your paint will keep indefinitely.

Artists' clear picture varnish. There is no hurry for this, as paintings should not be varnished in under six months' drying time.

WORK AREA

The ideal would be a room facing north but you will probably end up in a corner of any room that is spare, using electric light. It is really unimportant where you work as long as you have the space to move and are comfortable. After all, Michelangelo painted on his back with a candle strapped to his head for four years and you cannot do better than the Sistine Chapel!

Measurements for colour formulas

In a painting colour is most important — even more than the drawing. At the risk of sounding unartistic and homey, I have broken down colour into almost exact amounts, rather like a recipe. I am going to use spoons for measuring, as this helps to keep amounts uniform. Of course, this gives me qualms, as I have visions of paint actually being measured out with spoons. Don't. Just gauge it by eye. This naturally means the amounts are not level.

The illustration below shows the amounts used in colour mixtures.

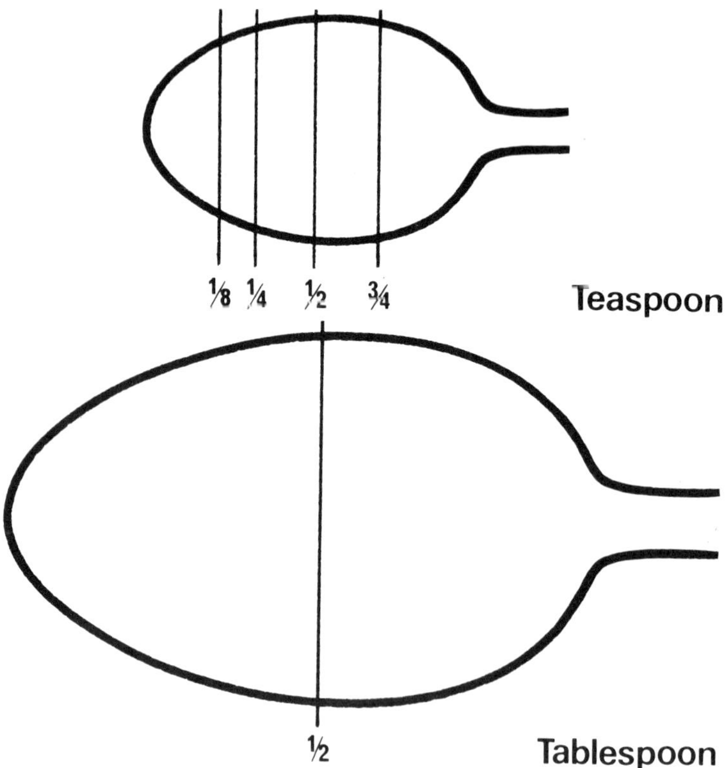

These amounts are geared mostly for knife painting which requires more paint, and ensure having the adequate amount of paint for each area in the painting. (You can use just as much paint by mixing in bits and dabs, which is both a nuisance and time-consuming.)

Keep your piles of mixed paint clean. If you have any mixed paint left over when you have finished a painting, remove the separate piles from the mixing area and arrange them in a neat line alongside the squeezed-out paints on the palette. Clean the mixing area, then cover the palette with polythene or tin foil and put it in the fridge or a cool, dark place. You can use left-over paint to work on a smaller canvas another time.

The colour formulas in this series can be used for other paintings as well. For instance, if you see a photograph or painting of a landscape that you would like to copy, use the colour formulas for San Juan Mountains, Colorado (on page 47) or Last Three in Totter-down (on page 64). Use a fairly good-sized photograph (for example from a calendar), or postcards, or even copy from the Impressionists such as Monet and Van Gogh. Cover the photograph or painting with a sheet of polythene, then, with a medium round brush and umber wash, draw in the grid lines and the picture, on the polythene, as shown in the drawings in this book. You can then transfer your drawing correctly on to canvas.

However, before you embark on this sort of experiment, finish the carefully chosen subjects in this book. In this way, you will feel more confident and courageous.

Painting procedures

1 Your first step is to cover the canvas with an umber wash. This gives the painting a richer colour and also allows you to wipe off the drawing if you make a mistake. To make the umber wash, squeeze out $\frac{1}{2}$ teaspoon burnt umber. Dip your large, flat hog brush into the turpentine or white spirit (it should not be dripping), and then into the burnt umber on the palette, pulling some aside to make a light, rather thin wash. Cover the canvas with the wash, taking care not to make it too dark or runny. Wipe the excess moisture with tissue but leave the canvas damp.

2 For the sectioning on the canvas use the medium round brush and umber wash. This time, use more burnt umber than turpentine or white spirit, in order to achieve a darker colour. If your canvas is to be used vertically, draw three vertical lines equally spaced and five horizontal lines. If your canvas is to be used horizontally, section it off with five equally spaced vertical lines and three horizontal lines (see the horizontal drawing on page 12 and the vertical drawing on page 22).

3 Put in the drawing reduced to simple form and the shading with the same dark umber wash and the medium round brush. Use tissue to erase, if necessary.

4 Set up your palette as shown in the photograph and key illustration on the following pages, using about a teaspoonful of each colour and mixing the aqua, purple and mixed green as instructed. The palette should be set up the same way each time and a copy of the set-up kept for reference.

5 Be accurate when mixing your colours. You may find that your colour mixtures vary slightly from the colour swatches shown in the book but this is normal. Just make sure that you keep the correct tonal values.

6 Keep your paint on your palette clean while working, by cleaning your knife before going from one colour to another.

7 Dabbling and stippling are two techniques you will find used in this book. To stipple

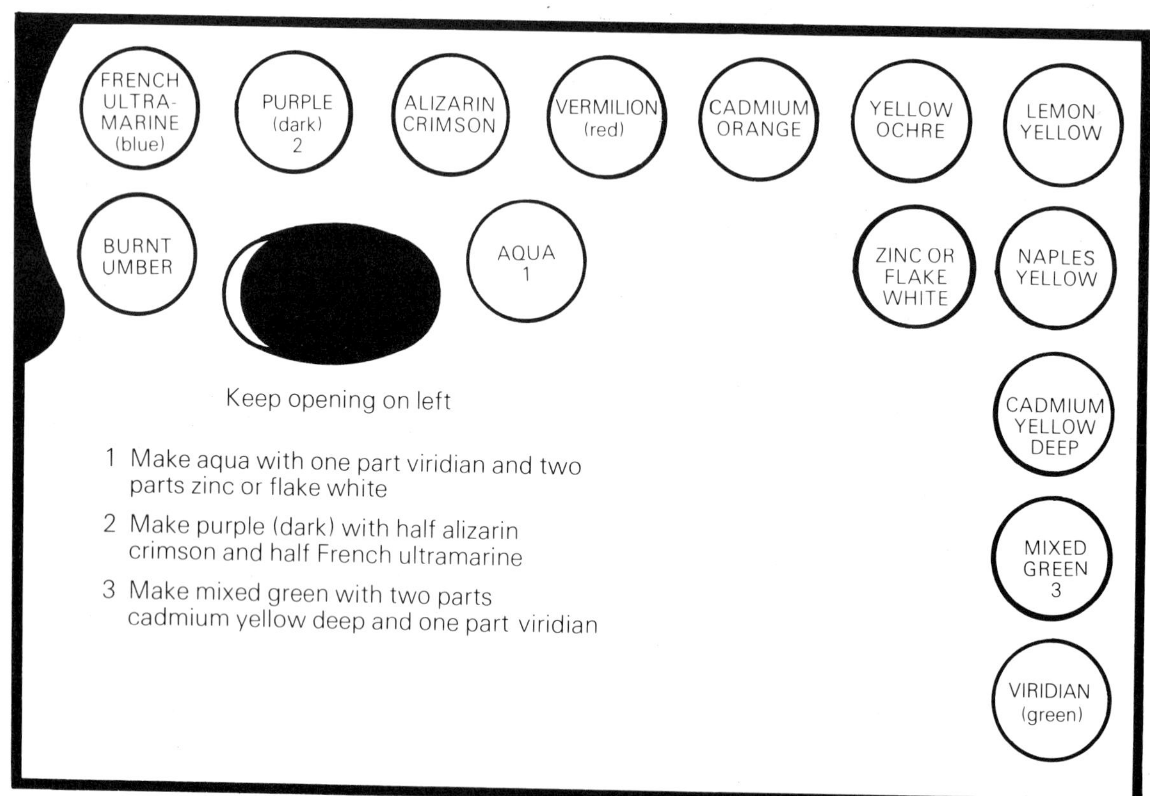

Set up your palette as shown above and opposite, using about a teaspoonful of each colour and mixing the aqua, purple and mixed green as instructed

colour on the canvas, put a small amount of paint on the tip of your knife or brush and cover the area required with short, sharp strokes to give a rough, raised texture. For dabbling, use a little more paint and, with the flat part of the top of the knife or brush, dab short strokes on the required area.

8 Six months after you have completed your painting, dust it off with a dry, soft paint brush and apply the clear varnish lightly. Lay the painting flat until dry — this will take about an hour.

9 One of the most difficult lessons to learn in painting is when to stop. You could argue that Albert P. Ryder, the famous American painter, reworked his paintings for thirty years in the solitude of his New York tenement. Painting over dust and grime gave a molten, jewel-like quality to his paintings. That's fine but, since it's quite possible that you may not be another Albert P. Ryder, forget it. In overworking, not only will your painting lose its spontaneity and freshness, but you may very well find that you lose the painting altogether.

The complete Nancy Kominsky Paint Along Outfit, illustrated opposite, has been made expressly to her specifications by George Rowney and Company Limited

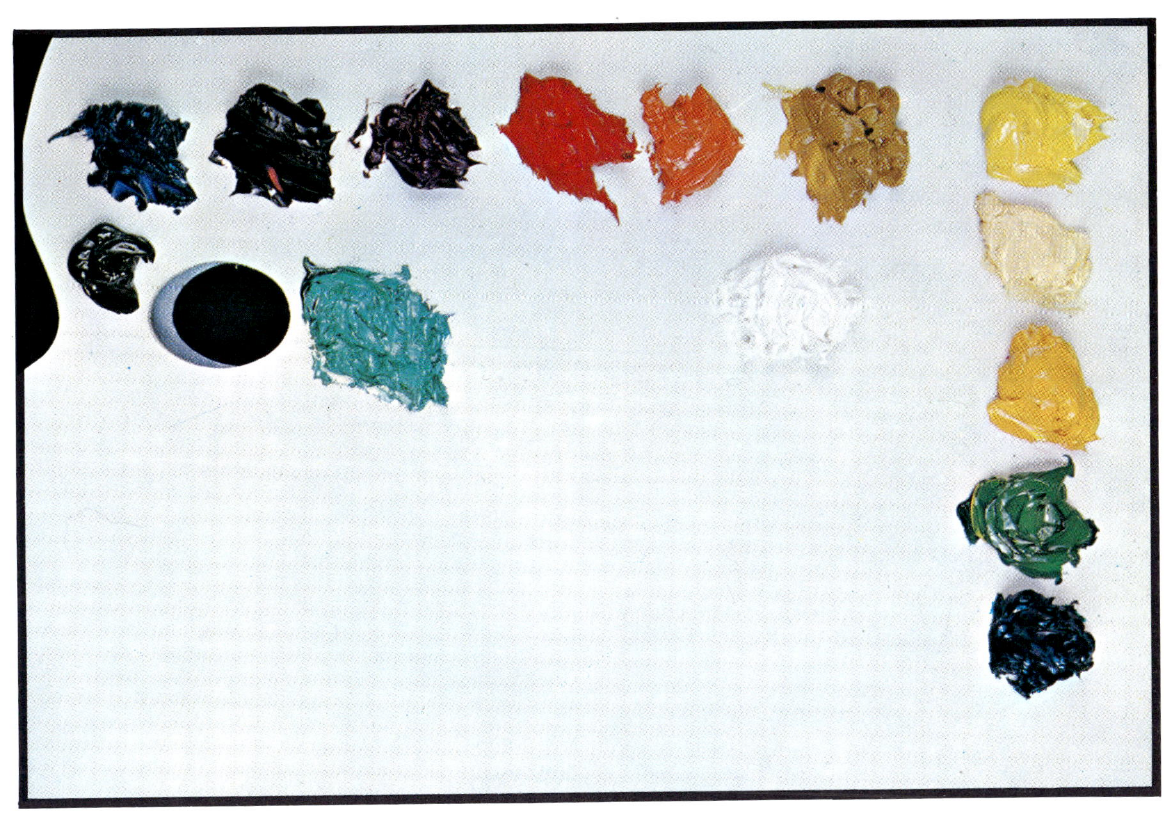

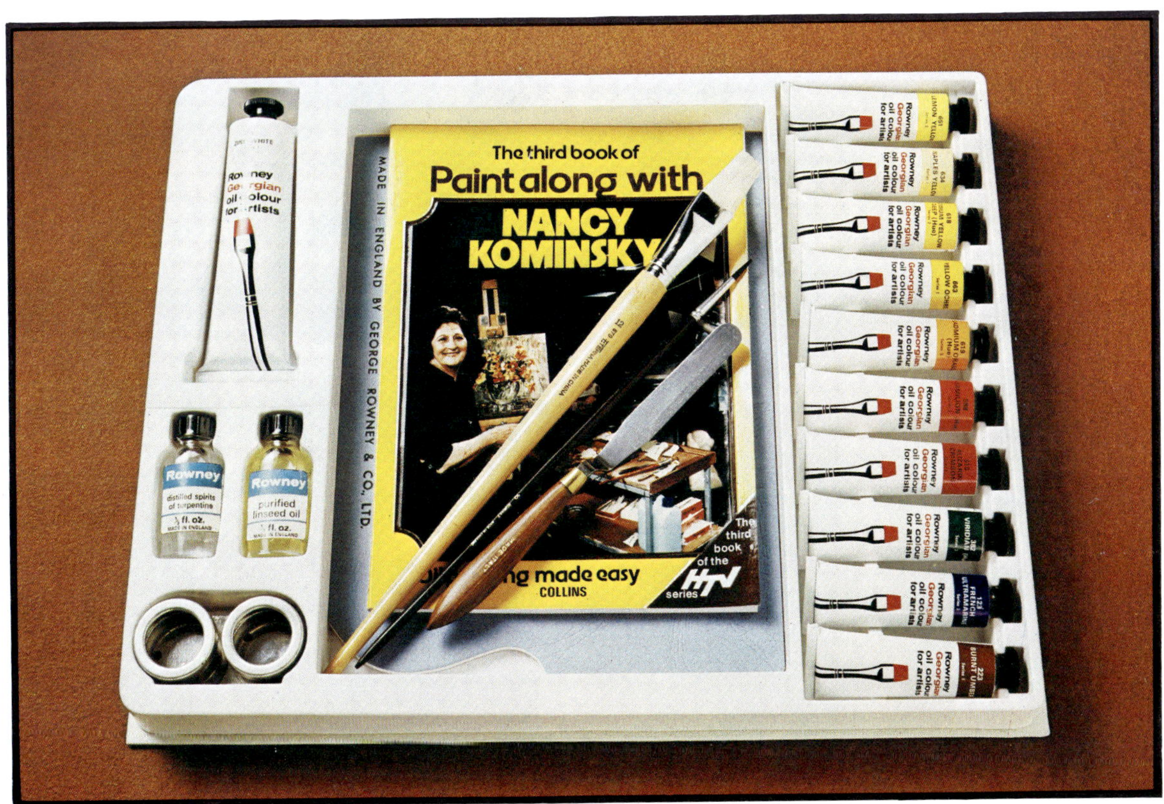

Rowney
Georgian
oil colour
for artists

Rowney
distilled spirits
of turpentine
½ fl. oz.
MADE IN ENGLAND

Rowney
purified
linseed oil
½ fl. oz.
MADE IN ENGLAND

The third book of
Paint along with
NANCY
KOMINSKY

ng made easy
COLLINS

The
third
book
of the
HTV
series

MADE IN ENGLAND BY GEORGE ROWNEY & CO., LTD.

Rowney
Georgian
oil colour
for artists

Anemones

Florals are best for beginners or if you haven't painted for a while.

THE DRAWING

1 Use canvas board, canvas or hardboard, 36cm (14 in.) by 46cm (18 in.) horizontally.
2 Study the drawing and painting on pages 12 and 13.
3 Arrange the palette according to the palette layout on page 8.
4 Use the large, flat hog brush to stain the canvas with a light wash of burnt umber, as described in Step 1 on page 7. Wipe with toilet tissue.
5 With the medium round brush and dark umber wash, put in the grid lines and simple drawing as indicated on page 12.
6 The light is coming from the right, so with dark umber wash lightly shade bowl and flowers where indicated.
7 Clean your brushes in the medium of turpentine or white spirit.

THE PAINTING

Always mix paints with straight knife.

BACKGROUND (always painted in first)

**Colour formula
Tones of white**

light　　　　　　　　medium　　　　　　　　dark

The procedure for mixing this colour is different from other methods.

Light tone
1¾ tablespoons white
¼ teaspoon Naples yellow
Mix and separate into three equal parts.
First part for light tone: do not touch

Second part for medium tone
add　**⅛ teaspoon burnt umber**
⅛ teaspoon aqua

Third part for dark tone
add　**¼ teaspoon burnt umber**
¼ teaspoon aqua
⅛ teaspoon yellow ochre

Clean your knife.

Let's paint
Use offset knife, held lightly.

1 Study the background in the painting on page 13.
2 Using the flat of the knife, paint the background in thirds of light, medium and dark tones, starting on the left with dark tone.
3 Blend tones slightly and go around flowers loosely. (The knife will feel awkward at first.) Clean knife.
4 Again with the flat of the knife, lightly stroke on purple where indicated on background, and underneath the bowl for shadows, using downward strokes. Lightly score the shadows horizontally with the tip of clean knife.
5 With the point of clean knife, scratch in wet paint any flowers lost.
6 Move left-over paint, if any, out of mixing area and clean the palette.
7 It is best to leave the background to dry before putting in flowers.

BOWL

Colour formula
Tones of white

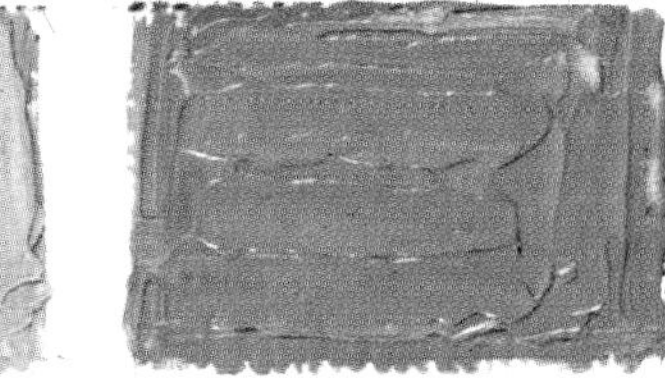

| light | medium | dark | extra dark |

Refer to the tones of white on the opposite page, used for the background and mix according to the directions. Mix the extra dark tone in the following way:

Extra dark tone
to $\frac{1}{2}$ teaspoon dark white tone
add $\frac{1}{8}$ teaspoon umber
$\frac{1}{8}$ teaspoon aqua
touch of alizarin crimson

1 Study the bowl in the painting on page 13.
2 With the flat of the knife paint circular strokes of dark tone on left side and bottom of bowl.
3 Again with circular strokes paint medium tone in the middle and light tone on the right side of bowl. Blend tones lightly.
4 Paint extra dark tone on left side and bottom of bowl where indicated. Blend lightly.
5 Outline the right side of bowl very lightly with extra dark tone.
6 Keep left-over tones of white for the white anemones which will be painted in later.

PURPLE ANEMONES

Colour formula
Tones of purple

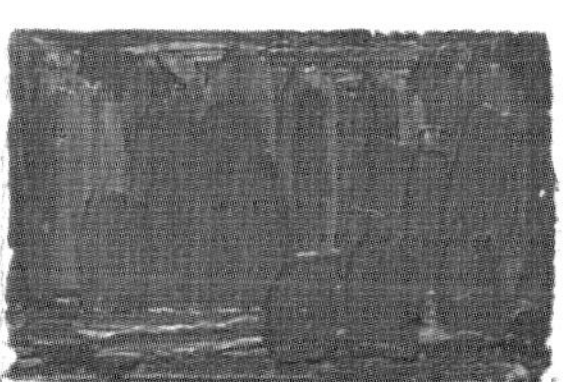

| light | medium | dark |

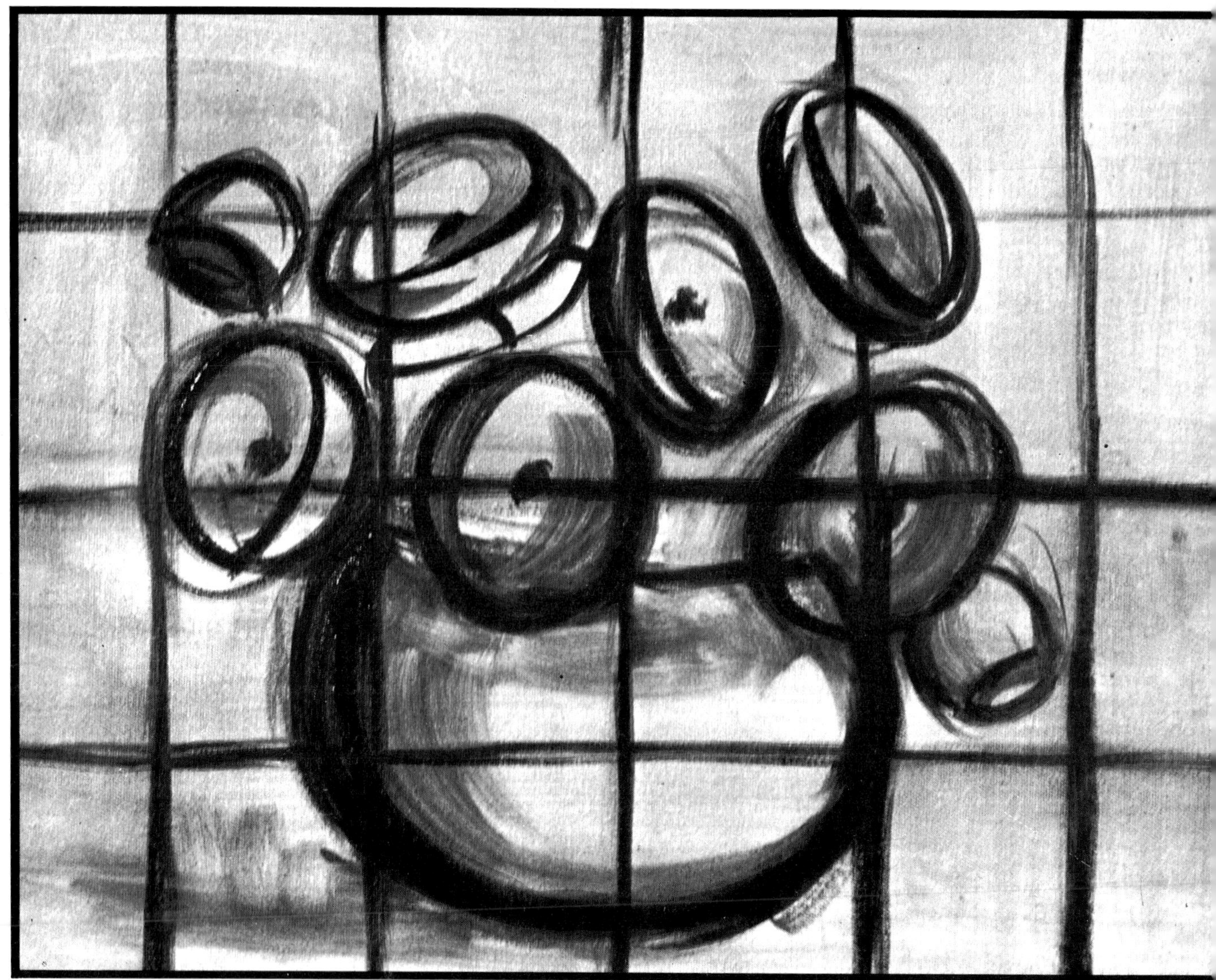

Medium tone
$\frac{3}{4}$ **tablespoon white**
$\frac{3}{4}$ **teaspoon purple**
$\frac{1}{8}$ **teaspoon blue**
Mix and separate into three parts, one small ($\frac{1}{2}$ teaspoon) and two equal parts.
First part ($\frac{1}{2}$ teaspoon) for light tone
add   1 teaspoon white
$\frac{1}{8}$ **teaspoon Naples yellow**
$\frac{1}{8}$ **teaspoon aqua**

Second part for medium tone: do not touch

Third part for dark tone
add   1 teaspoon purple
$\frac{1}{8}$ **teaspoon blue**

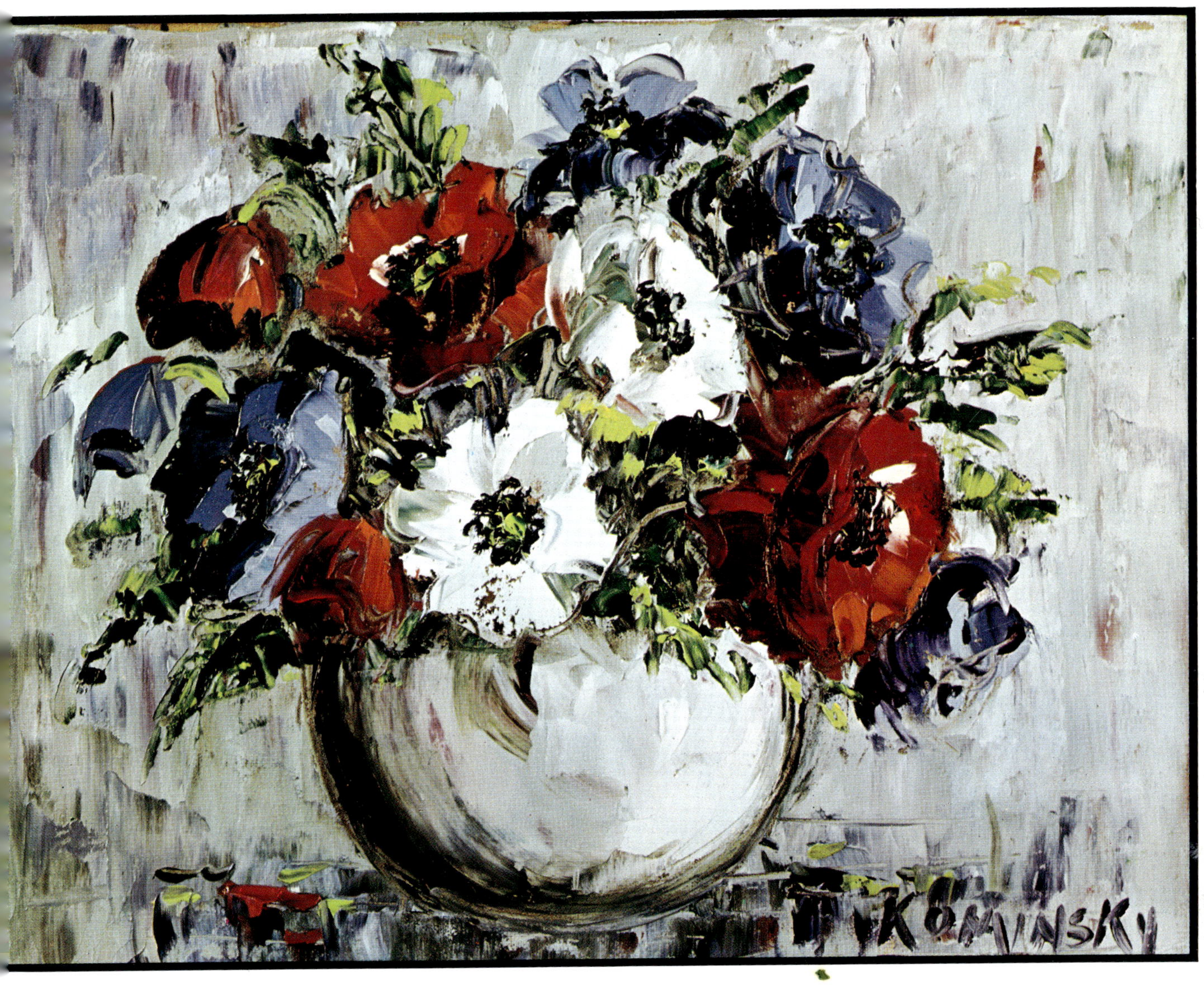

1 Study the purple anemones in the painting above. You will see that I have added three extra flowers.
2 Start with the flower at the top of the bunch. Paint the top petals with light tone and the lower petals with medium and dark tones. Always slant petals to the centre of the flower, using the flat of the knife.
3 Paint the open flower on the left with light tone on the right of it and medium and dark tones on the left.
4 Paint the unopened flower on the left with dark and medium tones. Outline the edge of the petals with purple from palette.
5 Paint the top petals of the flower on the upper right with light and medium tones, and the lower petals with dark and medium tones. Retain the loose feeling of the petals by scratching with the knife around the edges. Watch strokes.
6 Paint the lower right flower with medium and light tones edged with dark tone.
7 The stamens of all the flowers will be added later.

RED ANEMONES

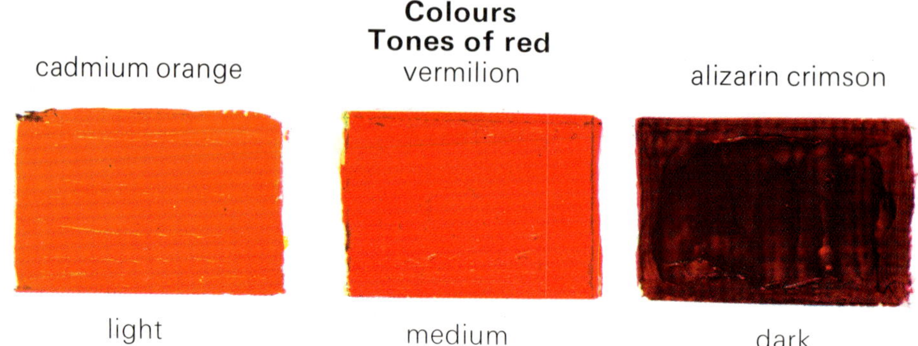

Colours
Tones of red

cadmium orange	vermilion	alizarin crimson
light	medium	dark

The above colours are used from the palette and require no mixing.

1 Study the red anemones in the painting on the previous page.
2 Paint the two unopened flowers with dark and medium tones, with a touch of light tone on the right edge of each. Outline the edge of petals with purple from palette.
3 Paint the top petals of the upper open flower with light and medium tones. Slant strokes to the centre.
4 Paint the shaded lower petals with medium and dark tones, then add dark and light tones to the outside of these petals.
5 Paint the lower petals of the flower on the right with light and medium tones.
6 Paint the shaded petals with dark and medium tones, adding touches of purple from palette where indicated.

WHITE ANEMONES

For these you will need the tones of white previously mixed for the bowl.

1 Study the white anemones in the painting on the previous page.
2 Paint all the petals of the large white flower in the centre foreground with light tone.
3 Using the flat of the knife paint short strokes of dark tone on the lower right petal and medium tone on the centre and left petals
4 Paint the petals of the flower directly above it with light and medium tones.
5 Add strokes of dark and medium tones on the left of the flower, where indicated.

LEAVES AND STAMENS

Colour formula
Tones of green

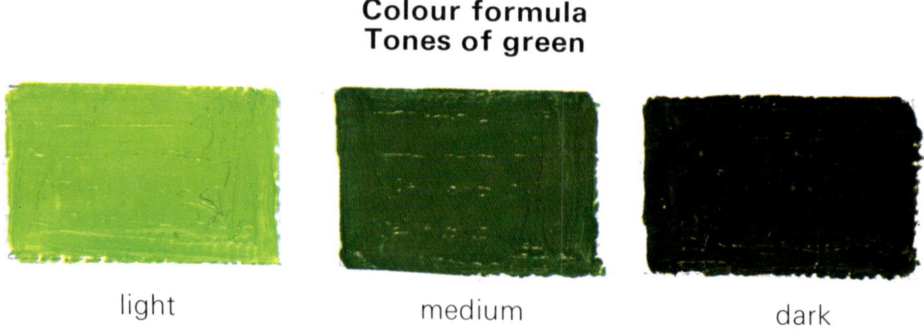

light	medium	dark

Medium tone
1 tablespoon mixed green
$\frac{1}{2}$ teaspoon yellow ochre
$\frac{1}{4}$ teaspoon vermilion
$\frac{1}{8}$ teaspoon cadmium orange

Mix and separate into three parts, one small ($\frac{1}{2}$ teaspoon) and two equal parts.
First part ($\frac{1}{2}$ teaspoon) for light tone
add   1 teaspoon white
1 teaspoon lemon yellow

Second part for medium tone: do not touch

Third part for dark tone
add $\frac{1}{4}$ teaspoon purple
$\frac{1}{2}$ teaspoon mixed green

1 Study the leaves in the painting on page 13. They are just a general impression. Do not paint too many.
2 Paint a few strokes of light, medium and dark tones between flowers.
3 Paint the leaves on the left side of flowers with medium and dark tones and tip them with light tone.
4 Paint the leaves on the right side of flowers with medium and light tones, adding the dark tone at the base of the leaves. Keep them lacy by using the tip of the knife.
5 For the stamens paint a round blob of medium green tone in the centre of each flower. Add a spot of light green tone on the right of each, for highlight.
6 Stipple dots of purple from palette unevenly around each blob.

HIGHLIGHTS AND FALLEN PETALS AND LEAVES
1 With medium white tone paint highlights on red anemones where indicated.
2 Paint a few fallen petals and leaves with medium and dark red tones, medium and light green tones and purple. Keep them delicate and do not paint too many.
3 Paint shadows under fallen petals and leaves with purple.

Now you've taken the plunge and I'm sure you are pleased with the result.

Strawberries

THE DRAWING

1 Use canvas board, canvas or hardboard, 36cm (14 in.) by 46cm (18 in.) horizontally.
2 Study the drawing and painting on pages 18 and 19.
3 Arrange the palette according to the palette layout on page 8.
4 Use the large, flat hog brush to stain the canvas with a light wash of burnt umber, as described in Step 1 on page 7. Wipe with toilet tissue.
5 With the medium round brush and dark umber wash put in the grid lines and simple drawing as indicated on page 18. Put the punnet in a box first. Watch perspective — you are looking down on it.
6 The light is coming from the left (note highlights on left side of punnet and berries), so with dark umber wash lightly shade right side of objects.
7 Clean your brushes in the medium of turpentine or white spirit.

THE PAINTING

Always mix paints with straight knife.

BACKGROUND

Colour formula
Tones of blue

 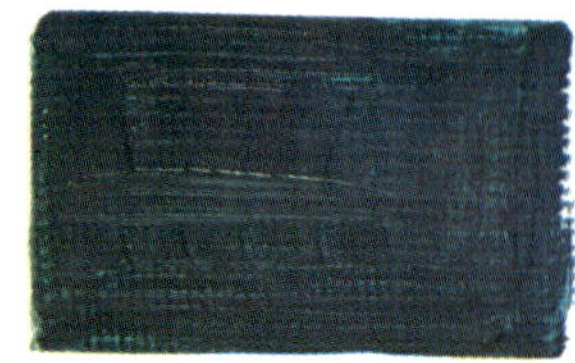 

light   medium   dark

Medium tone
1 teaspoon white
$\frac{3}{4}$ **teaspoon aqua**
$\frac{1}{2}$ **teaspoon blue**
$\frac{1}{4}$ **teaspoon cadmium orange**
$\frac{1}{8}$ **teaspoon mixed green**

Mix and separate into three parts, one small ($\frac{1}{2}$ teaspoon) and two equal parts.

First part ($\frac{1}{2}$ teaspoon) for light tone
add $\frac{3}{4}$ **teaspoon white**
       $\frac{1}{4}$ **teaspoon Naples yellow**
       $\frac{1}{2}$ **teaspoon aqua**

Second part for medium tone: do not touch

Third part for dark tone
add $\frac{1}{2}$ **teaspoon blue**
       $\frac{3}{4}$ **teaspoon aqua**
       $\frac{1}{2}$ **teaspoon cadmium orange**

Clean your knife.

Let's paint
Use offset knife, held lightly.

1 Study the background in the painting on page 19.
2 Using long, flat strokes, paint in the background, starting with dark tone on the right. Paint medium tone in the centre and light tone on the left. With clean knife scratch in any fruit lost in the painting.
3 Paint under objects with purple, to form shadows. Using the flat of the knife lightly drag the purple in downward strokes. Then, with the tip of clean knife, lightly scratch over this with horizontal strokes to make reflections.
4 Lightly stroke a little alizarin crimson and purple on the left of the background where indicated.

PUNNET

**Colour formula
Tones of yellow ochre**

light   medium   dark

**Medium tone
1 tablespoon yellow ochre
$\frac{1}{2}$ teaspoon white
$\frac{1}{2}$ teaspoon lemon yellow**

Mix and separate into three parts, one small ($\frac{1}{2}$ teaspoon) and two equal parts.

**First part ($\frac{1}{2}$ teaspoon) for light tone
add   1 teaspoon white
$\frac{1}{2}$ teaspoon lemon yellow**

Second part for medium tone: do not touch

**Third part for dark tone
add $\frac{1}{2}$ teaspoon purple**

1 Study the punnet in the painting on page 19.
2 Paint the right of the punnet with flat, downward strokes of dark tone, taking care to retain the lip.
3 Paint the middle of this righthand section with medium tone.
4 Paint a few strokes of light tone at the corner of the punnet. Blend tones lightly but do not lose the form.
5 Paint medium tone at the corner of the lefthand section of the punnet.
6 Paint the rest of the lefthand section with light tone, using the same strokes.
7 Outline the whole of the punnet and paint in the two centre horizontal lines with purple. Drag a few strokes of purple down on the right side, in shadow, and where indicated.

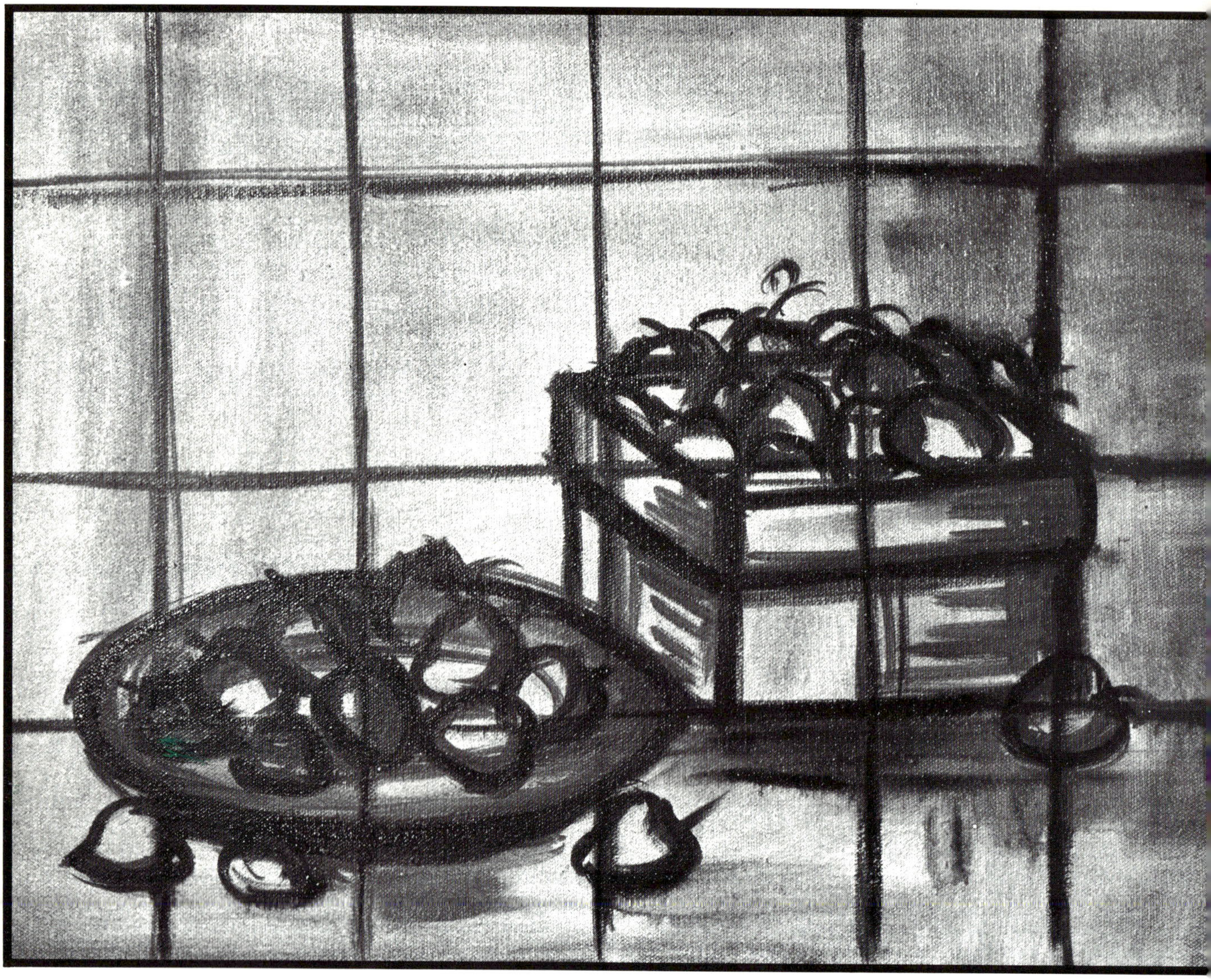

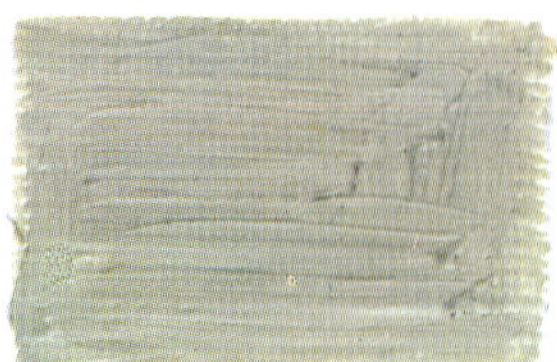

PLATE

**Colour formula
Tones of white**

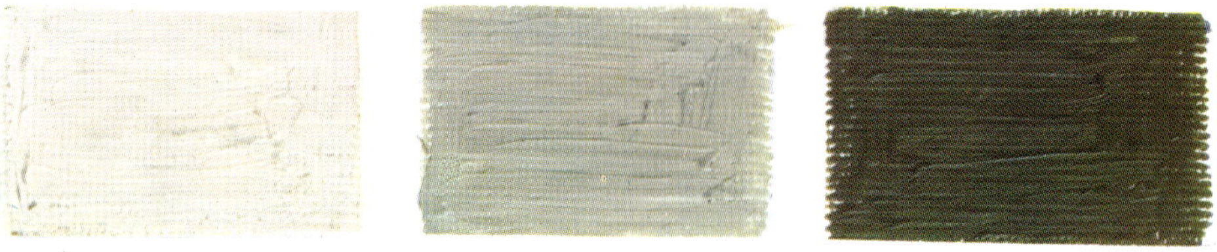

light   medium   dark

Refer to page 10 for tones of white and mix according to the directions.

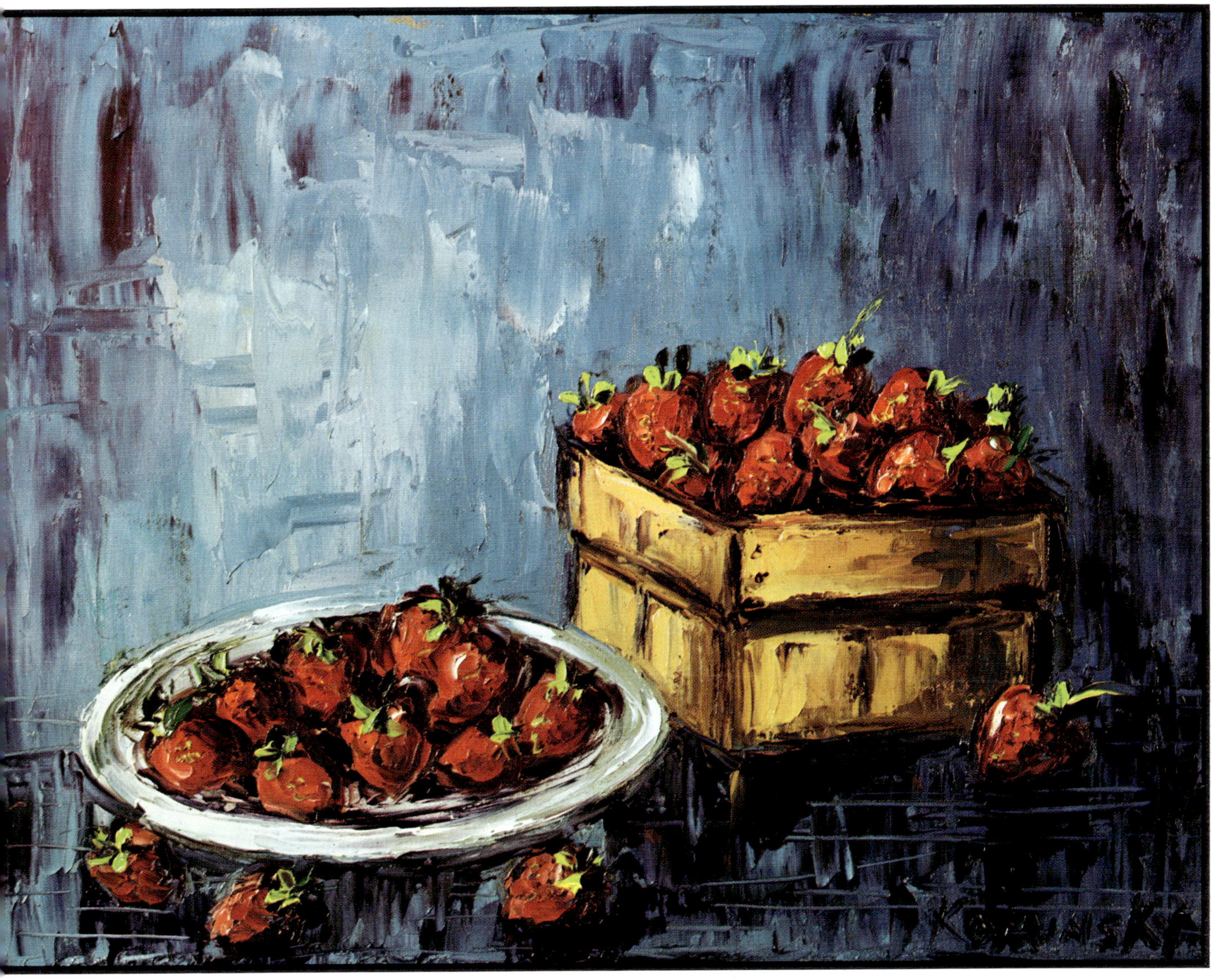

1 Study the plate in the painting above.
2 Paint dark tone in circular strokes underneath and around the fruit. Do not lose the shape of the plate.
3 Paint the remainder of the plate with medium tone, again using circular strokes. Blend tones lightly.
4 Paint light tone around the edge of the plate, for highlights.
5 Paint purple around and under fruit, for shadows.

STRAWBERRIES

**Colours
Tones of red**

cadmium orange   vermilion   alizarin crimson

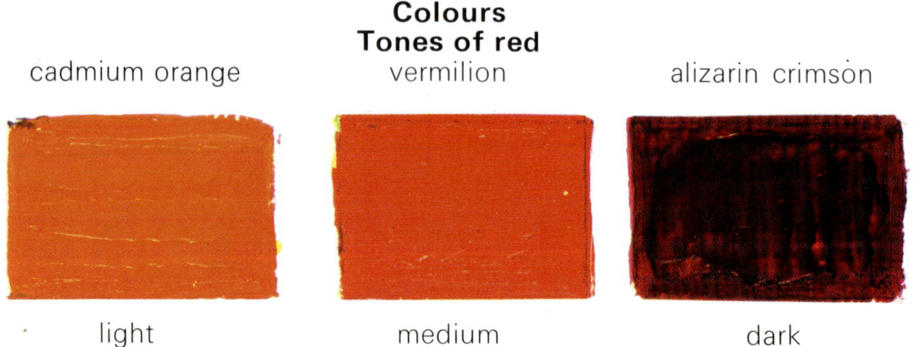

light   medium   dark

The above colours are used from the palette and require no mixing. However, you will need an additional tone which you mix in the following way:

**Extra light tone
$\frac{1}{2}$ teaspoon cadmium orange
$\frac{1}{2}$ teaspoon vermilion
$\frac{1}{8}$ teaspoon cadmium yellow deep
$\frac{3}{4}$ teaspoon white**

1 Study the strawberries in the painting on the previous page.
2 Using stippling strokes paint dark tone on the right side of the strawberries, taking care not to lose their shape. Keep them separated by lightly outlining the right side of each with purple.
3 Stipple medium tone in the centre of the strawberries and light tone on the left. Blend lightly.
4 Stipple a few strokes of extra light tone on each strawberry, for highlight.

LEAVES AND STEMS

**Colour formula
Tones of green**

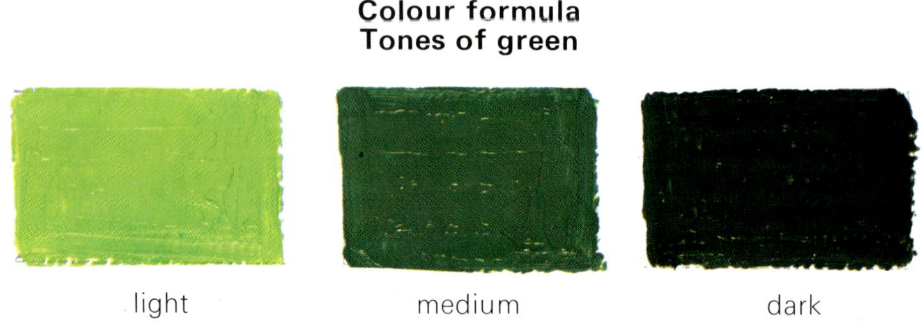

light   medium   dark

Refer to page 14 for tones of green and mix according to the directions.

1 Study the painting on the previous page. The leaves on each strawberry form a circle.
2 Paint the leaves on the right with dark and medium tones. Do not make them too large.
3 Paint the leaves on the left with light tone.
4 Paint the stems in the centre of each circle of leaves with dark tone. Keep them indefinite.

I'm sure your strawberries look good enough to eat!

Snow in Central Park

THE DRAWING

1 Use canvas board, canvas or hardboard, 36cm (14 in.) by 46cm (18 in.) vertically.
2 Study the drawing and painting on pages 22 and 23.
3 Arrange the palette according to the palette layout on page 8.
4 Use the large, flat hog brush to stain the canvas with a light wash of burnt umber, as described in Step 1 on page 7. Wipe with toilet tissue.
5 With the medium round brush and dark umber wash put in the grid lines and simple drawing as indicated on page 22. Draw general box-like forms for buildings first for correct placement and size, then put them in perspective as indicated. Do not draw in windows. I suggest you practise drawing the buildings on paper first.
6 The light is coming from the left, so with dark umber wash lightly shade the areas on the right side of buildings and where indicated.
7 Clean your brushes in the medium of turpentine or white spirit.

THE PAINTING

SKY

Colour formula
Tones of greyed light green

| light | medium | dark |

Medium tone
1½ tablespoons white
1 teaspoon yellow ochre
½ teaspoon mixed green
⅛ teaspoon vermilion

Mix and separate into three parts, one small (½ teaspoon) and two equal parts.

First part (½ teaspoon) for light tone
add   ¾ teaspoon white
⅛ teaspoon yellow ochre

Second part for medium tone: do not touch

Third part for dark tone
add   ¼ teaspoon purple
¼ teaspoon mixed green

You will need an additional tone, which you mix in the following way:

Extra light tone
to   ¼ teaspoon light greyed light green tone
add   ¾ teaspoon white
⅛ teaspoon Naples yellow

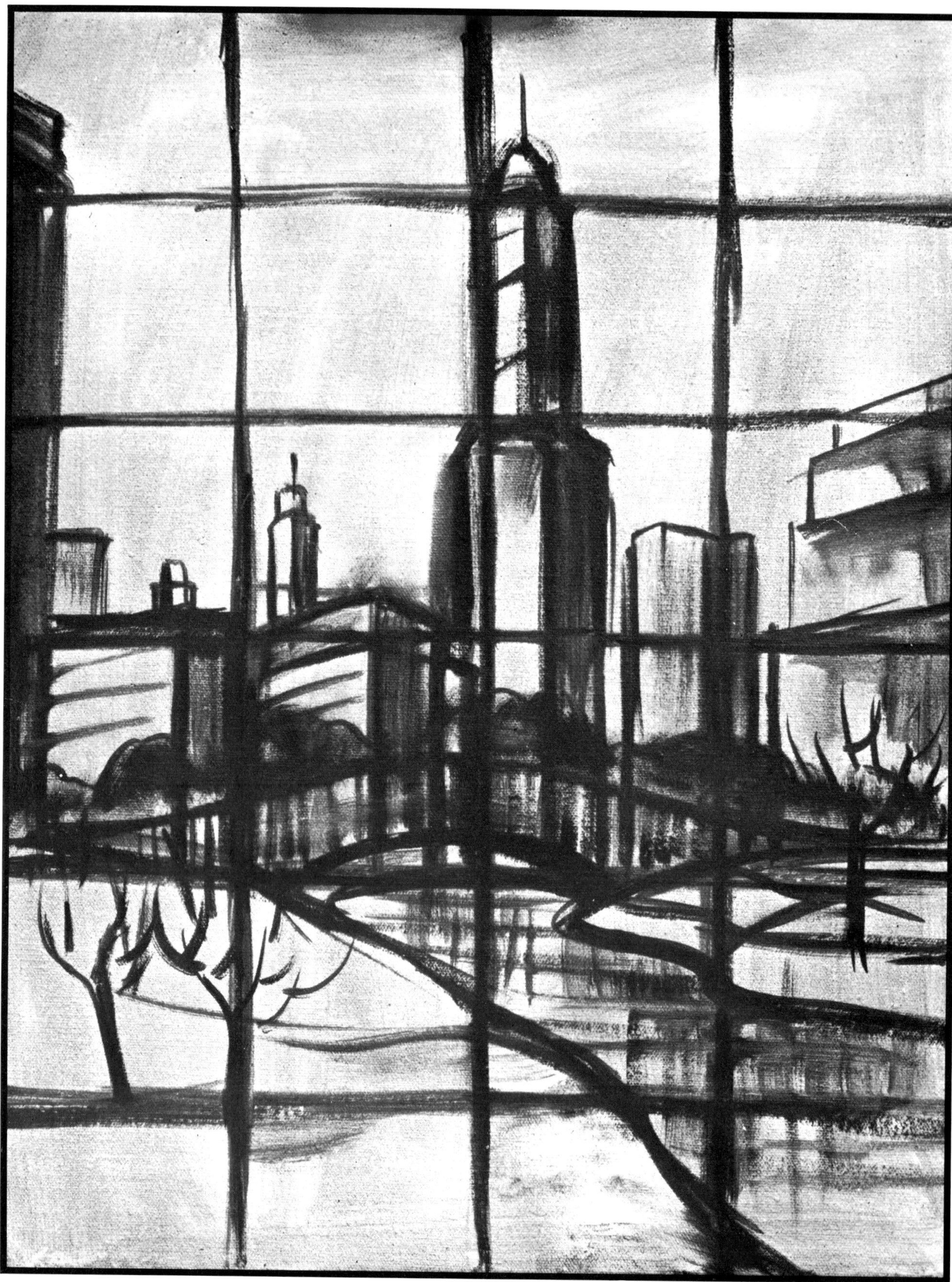

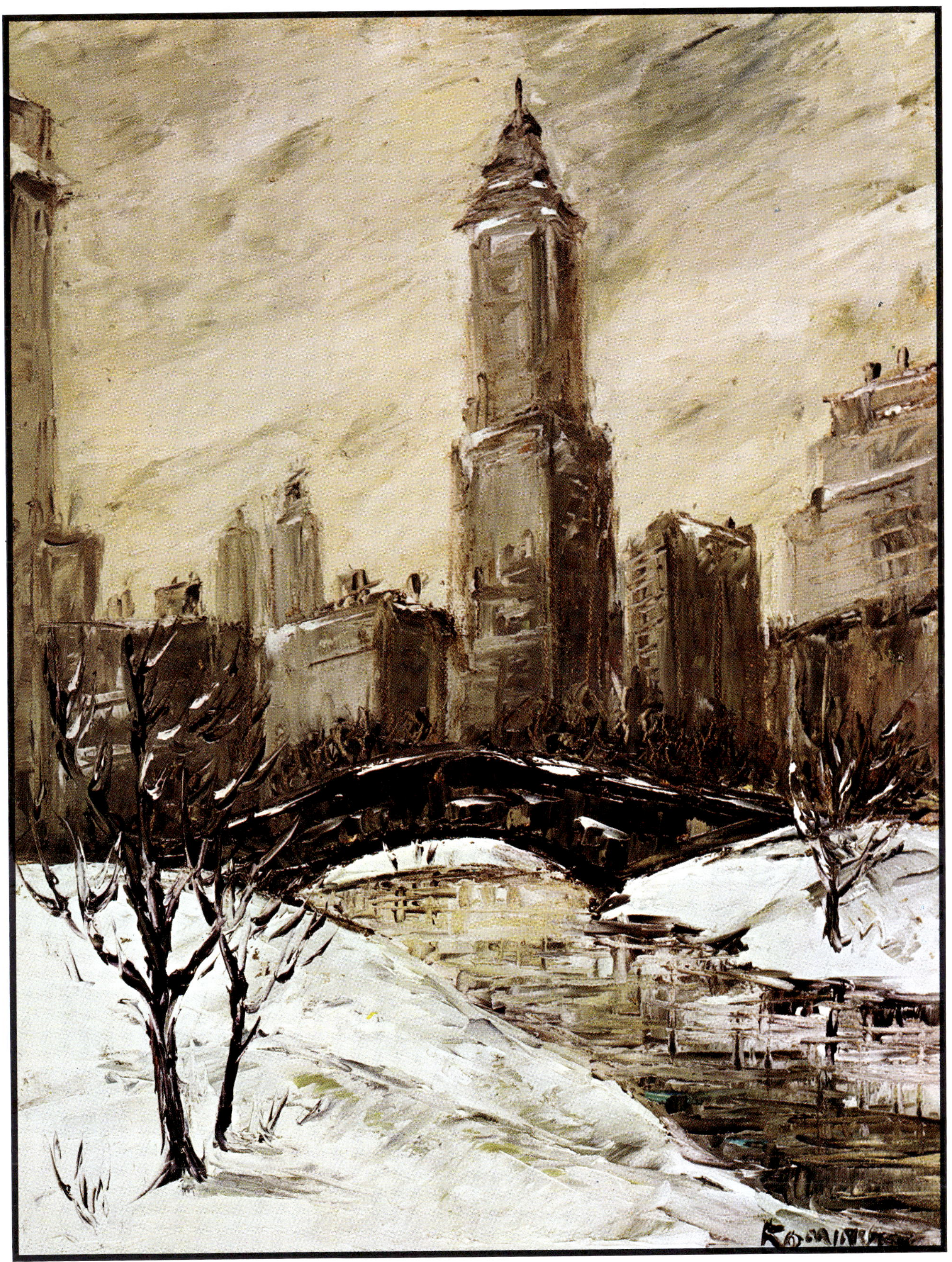

Clean your knife.

Let's paint
Use offset knife, held lightly.

1 Study the sky in the painting on the previous page.
2 Paint extra light tone carefully around the tops of the buildings and up into the sky.
3 Paint light tone above it in flat, slanting strokes.
4 Paint medium tone at the top of the canvas, blending with a little dark tone, again in slanting, sweeping strokes. Blend slightly, taking care not to lose tonal values.

BUILDINGS

In addition to the greyed light green tones, you will need three tones which you mix in the following way:

A   to $\frac{1}{2}$ teaspoon light greyed light green tone
add   touch of purple
touch of blue

B   to $\frac{1}{2}$ teaspoon medium greyed light green tone
add $\frac{1}{8}$ teaspoon purple
touch of blue

C   to $\frac{3}{4}$ teaspoon dark greyed light green tone
add $\frac{1}{4}$ teaspoon purple
touch of blue
touch of alizarin crimson

1 Study the buildings in the painting on the previous page.
2 Paint the building on the extreme left of the canvas, the one on the left of the tower and the one on the extreme right of the canvas with light tone A.
3 Paint the shaded areas of these buildings with long, flat strokes of dark tone C.
4 Paint the second building from the left of the canvas and the building on the right of the tower with medium tone B.
5 Paint the shaded areas of these buildings with dark tone C. Watch perspective.
6 The tower is painted in three sections. Paint the upper section with light tone A on the left and dark tone C on the right, in shadow. Paint the left of the lower section with medium tone B and the right with dark tone C, in shadow. Paint the top of the tower with light tone A and add a few touches of dark tone C, for definition.
7 Paint the two small towers on the left of the tower with the original medium greyed light green tone. Add a touch of dark tone C at the top.
8 With clean knife score in the angles of the buildings and an impression of windows. Paint in a few chimneys with dark tone C.
9 Lightly paint a few strokes of purple at the base of all the buildings.

BRIDGE (no detail please)
1 Study the bridge in the painting on the previous page.
2 Paint short, downward strokes of dark greyed light green tone in the shape of the bridge.
3 Blend in strokes of purple, again using short, downward strokes.
4 Outline the whole of the bridge with purple.

WATER
For this you will need the light greyed light green tone used for the sky, together with tones B and C used for the buildings.

1 Study the water in the painting on page 23.
2 Paint the water under the bridge with horizontal strokes of light greyed light green tone.
3 Paint the rest of the water first with medium tone B and then with dark tone C.
4 Paint strokes of purple in the water where indicated. Outline the shoreline with purple.
5 With point of clean knife score water with a few vertical strokes, for reflections.
6 Add a couple of touches of aqua.

SNOW

**Colour formula
Tones of white**

light   medium   dark

Refer to page 10 for tones of white and mix according to the directions.

1 Study the snow in the painting on page 23.
2 Paint the right side of both mounds with dark and medium tones.
3 Paint the left side of the mounds with light tone. Blend lightly.
4 Paint the small area of snow under the bridge with light tone.
5 Paint a few horizontal strokes of light tone in the water to give reflections of snow.

TREES (You may use round brush)
1 Study the trees in the painting on page 23.
2 Paint the small tree on the right of the canvas with purple. Keep it delicate.
3 Paint the larger trees on the left with purple. Scratch in a tiny bush in the snow with the point of the knife.
4 Paint a little light white tone on bridge, buildings and trees, to give an impression of snow. Do not use too much paint.

This is not an easy painting but it is well worth the effort — it may be your favourite.

Twilight in the Cotswolds

THE DRAWING

1 Use canvas board, canvas or hardboard, 36cm (14 in.) by 46cm (18 in.) vertically.
2 Study the drawing and painting on pages 28 and 29.
3 Arrange the palette according to the palette layout on page 8.
4 Use the large, flat hog brush to stain the canvas with a light wash of burnt umber, as described in Step 1 on page 7. Wipe with toilet tissue.
5 With the medium round brush and dark umber wash put in the grid lines and simple drawing as indicated on page 28. Study carefully the curve of the path to the house.
6 The light is coming from the right, so with dark umber wash lightly shade the left side of the house and where indicated.
7 Clean your brushes in the medium of turpentine or white spirit.

THE PAINTING

SKY

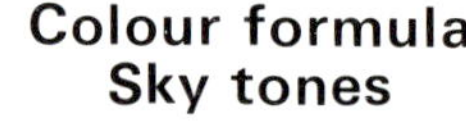

**Colour formula
Sky tones**

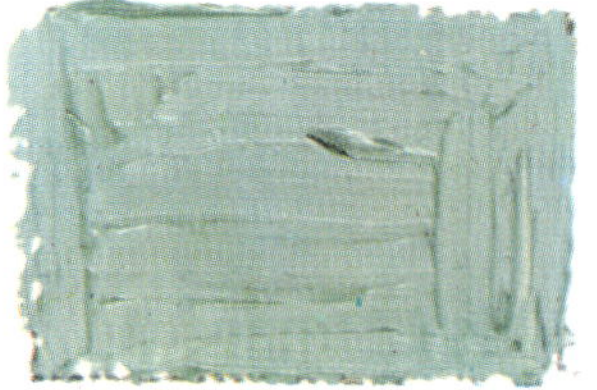  

light   medium   dark

Medium tone
1 tablespoon white
$\frac{1}{8}$ teaspoon aqua
$\frac{1}{4}$ teaspoon blue
$\frac{1}{4}$ teaspoon cadmium orange

Mix and separate into three parts, one small ($\frac{1}{2}$ teaspoon) and two equal parts.

First part ($\frac{1}{2}$ teaspoon) for light tone
add   1 teaspoon white
$\frac{3}{4}$ teaspoon Naples yellow

Second part for medium tone: do not touch

Third part for dark tone
add $\frac{1}{8}$ teaspoon blue
$\frac{1}{4}$ teaspoon aqua
$\frac{1}{4}$ teaspoon cadmium orange
$\frac{1}{8}$ teaspoon purple

Clean your knife.

In this painting only the light and medium tones are used for the sky. The dark tone is used for the house, path and large tree.

Let's paint
Use offset knife, held lightly.

1 Study the sky in the painting on page 29.
2 Paint light tone around the tops of the trees at the back of the house and up into the sky a little. Paint out the top of the large tree for now.
3 Paint the remaining sky area with medium tone and blend slightly where tones meet. Do not lose tonal values and take care to retain light tone around the trees.

HOUSE

Colour tones
First part for dark tone
to   **dark sky tone**
add $\frac{1}{4}$ **teaspoon purple**
     $\frac{1}{8}$ **teaspoon cadmium orange**
     $\frac{1}{4}$ **teaspoon white**
     touch of aqua
Mix and separate into two equal parts.
Second part for light tone
add $\frac{1}{2}$ **teaspoon white**
     $\frac{1}{2}$ **teaspoon Naples yellow**
     touch of cadmium orange

1 Study the house in the painting on page 29.
2 Paint dark and light tones alternately on the right half of the roof to create slates. Outline the edge of the roof with purple.
3 Paint the roof of the dormer window and the window with purple.
4 Paint the front of the house with dark and light tones. Add a few touches of light sky tone on the right.
5 Paint the small extension of the house with purple from palette and light tone on the right edge.
6 Paint the window on this extension with dark tone, then add lines of Naples yellow for window frames.
7 Paint the small half-round windows on the front of the house with purple. Keep the right side of each window lighter. (No black holes.)
8 Paint the door with purple from palette on the right side and medium sky tone on the left.
9 Paint the canopy over the doorway with light tone used for the house, edged with Naples yellow.
10 Add a few touches of medium sky tone over the lefthand window.
11 Keep left-over tones used for the house for the chimneys which will be painted later.

THATCHED ROOFS

Colour formula
Tones of yellow ochre

light

medium

dark

Refer to page 17 for tones of yellow ochre and mix according to the directions.

1 Study the thatched roofs in the painting on page 29.

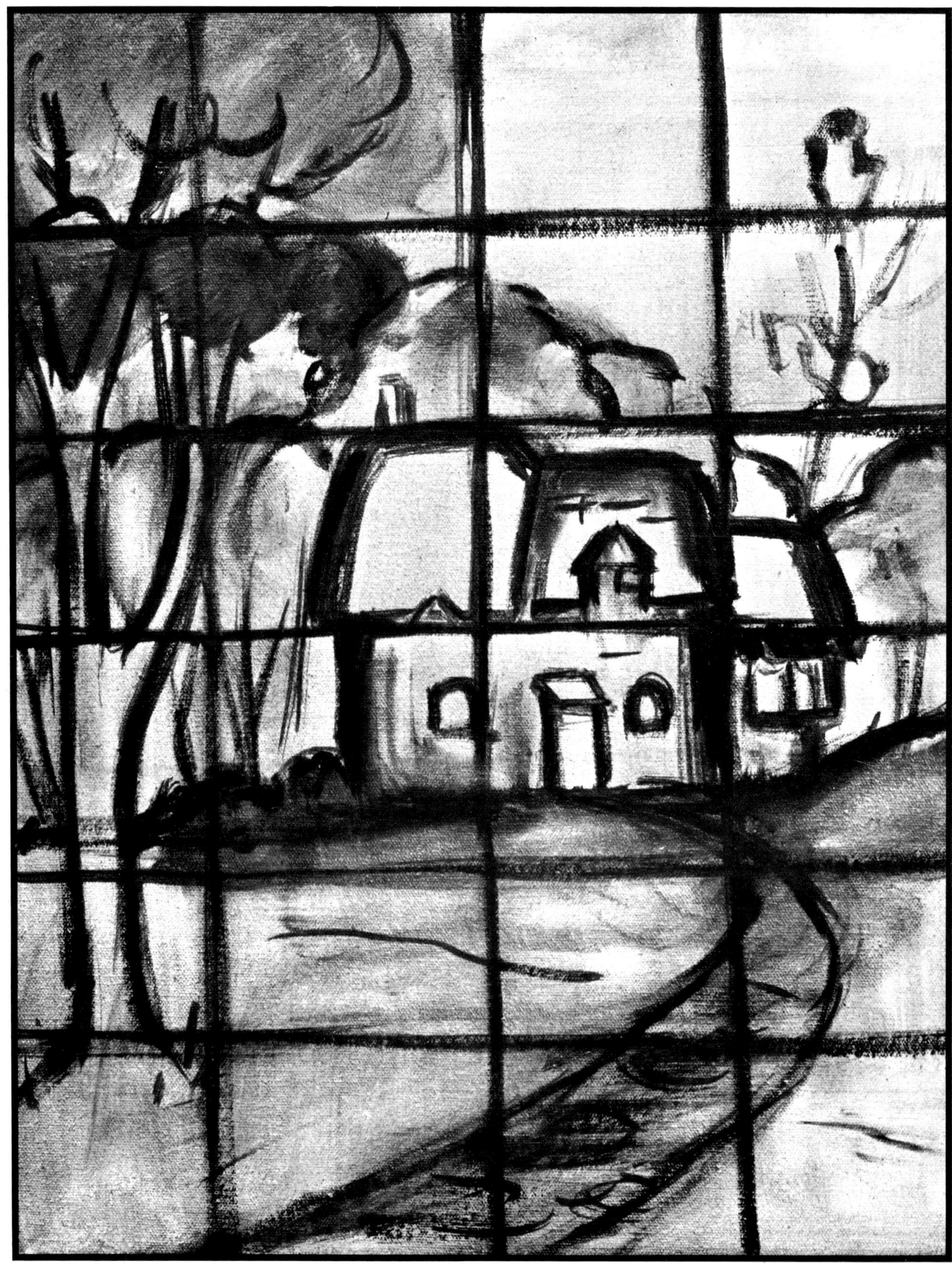

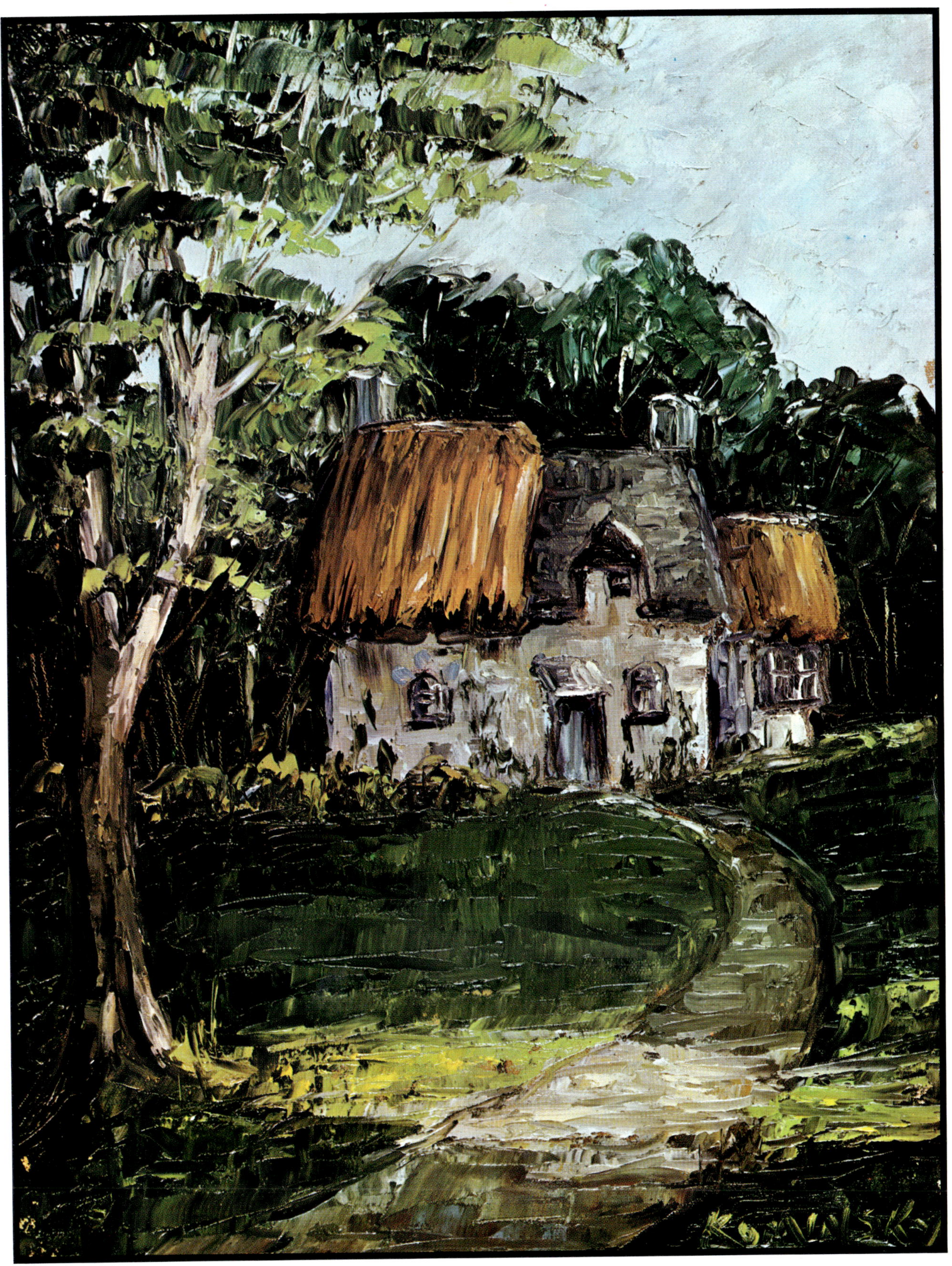

2 Paint dark tone on the left of the roofs, medium tone in the centre and light tone on the right. Create a texture of thickness with the paint.
3 Paint a few strokes of purple on the left of the thatched roofs and underneath them to create shadows and depth.

PATH
1 Study the path in the painting on the previous page.
2 Paint the area of the path down to and after the ray of light with dark tone used for the house.
3 Paint the ray of light with light tone used for the house.
4 Outline the right edge of the path with purple. Blend tones lightly.

TREES, GRASS AND SHRUBS

**Colour formula
Tones of green**

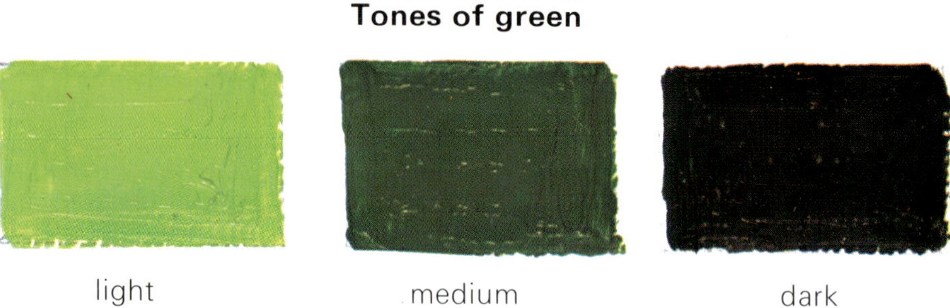

light   medium   dark

Refer to page 14 for tones of green and mix according to the directions. Then use these green tones to make up the following three tones:

Light tone
to **light green tone**
add $\frac{1}{8}$ **teaspoon yellow ochre**
touch of vermilion
touch of cadmium orange

Medium tone
to **medium green tone**
add $\frac{1}{8}$ **teaspoon vermilion**
$\frac{1}{4}$ **teaspoon white**
touch of cadmium orange

Dark tone
to **dark green tone**
add $\frac{1}{4}$ **teaspoon purple**
$\frac{1}{8}$ **teaspoon vermilion**

1 Study the trees, grass and shrubs in the painting on the previous page.
2 Paint the mass of trees at the back of the house starting with dark tone directly above the roof, then medium tone and finish with light tone. Use half circular strokes and create separate masses by adding a few touches of vermilion to one or two. Bring the dark tone down to the grass at the back of the house.
3 Blend purple into the dark tone at the base of the trees, for depth.
4 Paint the area of grass on the left of the path up to the ray of light with medium tone on the right and dark tone on the left.
5 Paint the area on the right of the path up to the ray of light with medium tone and touches of dark tone, then paint along the edge of the path with dark tone.
6 Paint the foreground in front of the ray of light on both sides of the path with dark

tone. The light green area will be painted later.
7 Paint the shrubs around the house with dark tone on the left and light tone on the right. Keep them small.
8 With clean knife scratch in the trunks and branches of the trees at the back of the house.

LARGE TREE
1 Study the trunk and branches of the large tree on the left of the painting on page 29.
2 Paint trunk and large branches with light tone used for the house.
3 Paint Naples yellow on branches and trunk where indicated.
4 Outline the left side of the tree with purple.

FOLIAGE AND HIGHLIGHTS

**Colour formula
Tones of green**

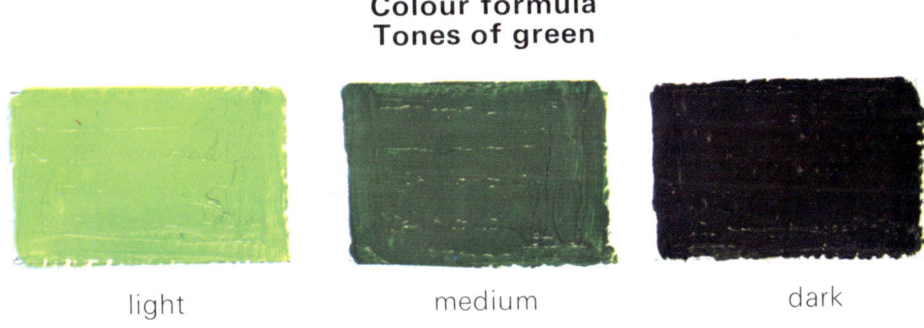

light   medium   dark

Refer to page 14 for tones of green and mix according to the directions.

1 Study the tree in the painting on page 29.
2 Paint stippling strokes of dark, medium and light tones across the tree as indicated. Keep light tones on the right of the tree.
3 Paint the light area of grass on either side of the path with light tone. Add a few touches of lemon yellow.
4 Paint short, horizontal strokes of Naples yellow on the path in this lighted area.
5 Paint the chimneys on the house with the dark and light tones used for the house.

This is an unusual study of dramatic light and shadow.

Nasturtiums

THE DRAWING

1 Use canvas board, canvas or hardboard, 36cm (14 in.) by 46cm (18 in.) horizontally.
2 Study the drawing and painting on pages 34 and 35.
3 Arrange the palette according to the palette layout on page 8.
4 Use the large, flat hog brush to stain the canvas with a light wash of burnt umber, as described in Step 1 on page 7. Wipe with toilet tissue.
5 With the medium round brush and dark umber wash put in the grid lines and simple drawing as indicated on page 34.
6 The light is coming from the right (note light on lower petals), so with dark umber wash lightly shade in areas on upper part of flowers, and the bowl as indicated.
7 Clean your brushes in the medium of turpentine or white spirit.

THE PAINTING

BACKGROUND

**Colour formula
Tones of greyed light green**

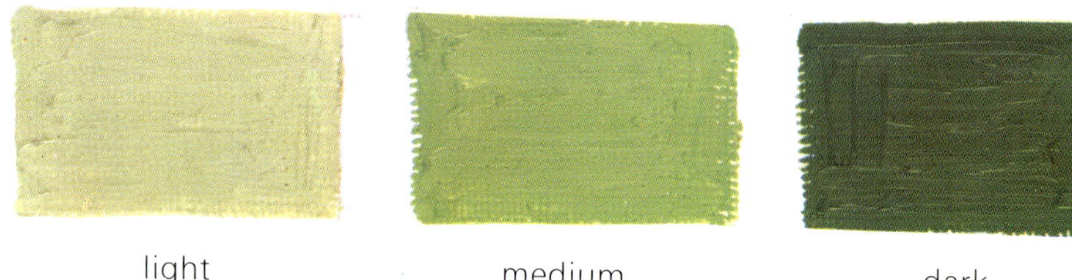

Refer to page 21 for tones of greyed light green and mix according to the directions.

Clean your knife.

Let's paint
Use offset knife, held lightly.

1 Study the background in the painting on page 35. The glass bowl will be painted in the same tones as the background.
2 Paint in the background starting with the dark tone on the left. Go through half of the bowl with the dark tone, but leave the outline of the bowl.
3 Paint medium tone in the middle of the canvas and through the other half of the bowl, leaving the outline.
4 Paint light tone on the right of the canvas, blending lightly.
5 To make the dark tone for the area between the flowers, the outline of the bowl and the shading, mix the following:

> **to** $\frac{1}{2}$ teaspoon dark greyed light green tone
> **add** $\frac{1}{4}$ teaspoon purple

6 Using the above tone, paint between the flowers, taking care not to lose them. Then paint into the bowl a little.
7 Paint the outline of the bowl carefully with this same tone.
8 Using the flat of the knife, paint this same tone under the bowl, dragging it down. Scratch in a few horizontal strokes for reflections.

NASTURTIUMS

These are vari-coloured flowers and painted slightly differently from others.

Colours
Tones of yellow

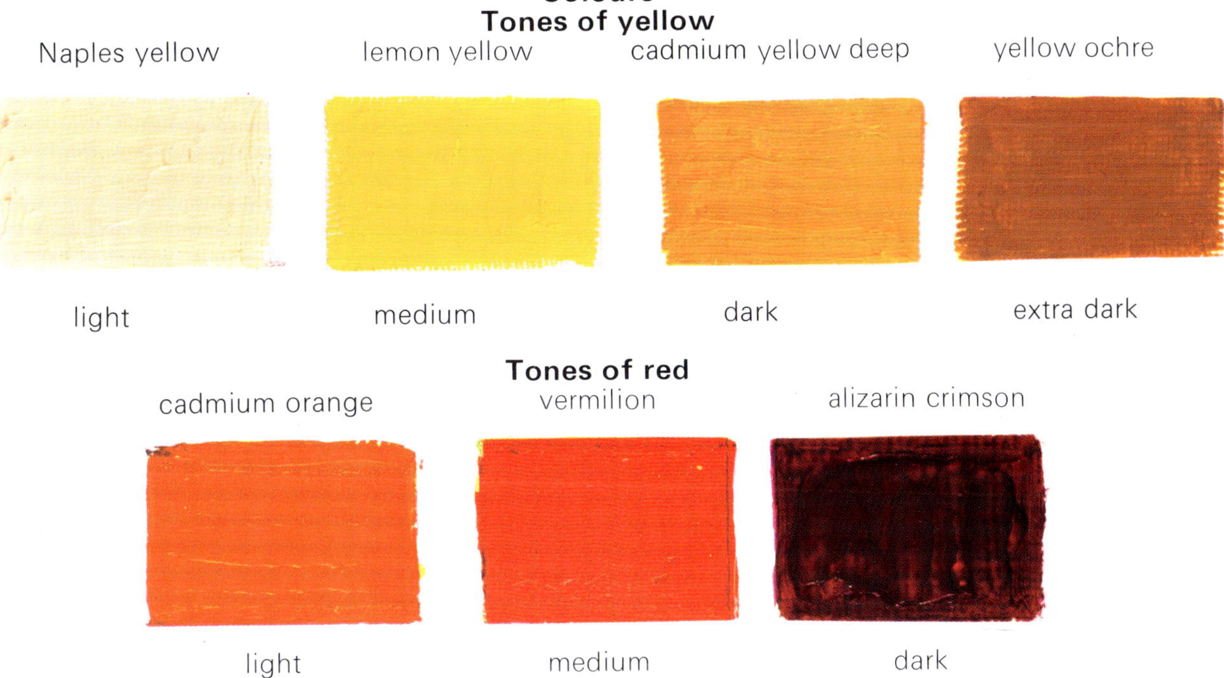

The above colours, tones of yellow and tones of red, are used from the palette and require no mixing.

1 Study the nasturtiums in the painting on page 35.
2 Because the colours are unmixed and each flower is made up of at least two colours, study the red, yellow and orange combinations in the painting and paint accordingly. Take care to maintain the character of the flowers — they must be nasturtiums.
3 Paint strokes of medium and dark red tones into the background, where indicated.

LEAVES AND STEMS

Colour formula
Tones of green

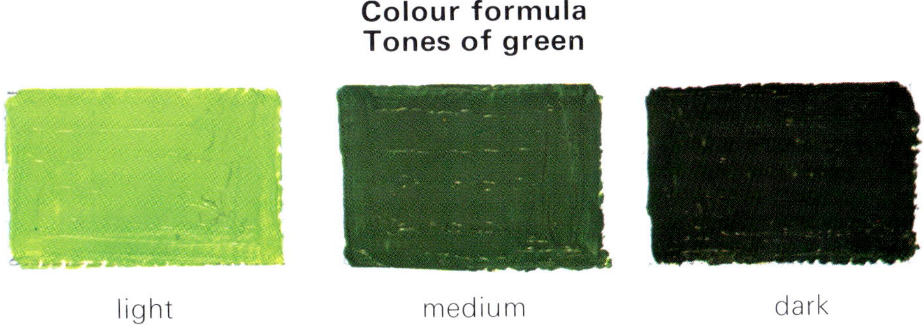

Refer to page 14 for tones of green and mix according to the directions.

1 Study the leaves in the painting on page 35. They are a distinctive round shape.
2 Paint blobs of dark, medium and light tones in between flowers.
3 Paint a few round leaves on the left with dark and medium tones.
4 Paint a few round leaves on the right with light and medium tones.

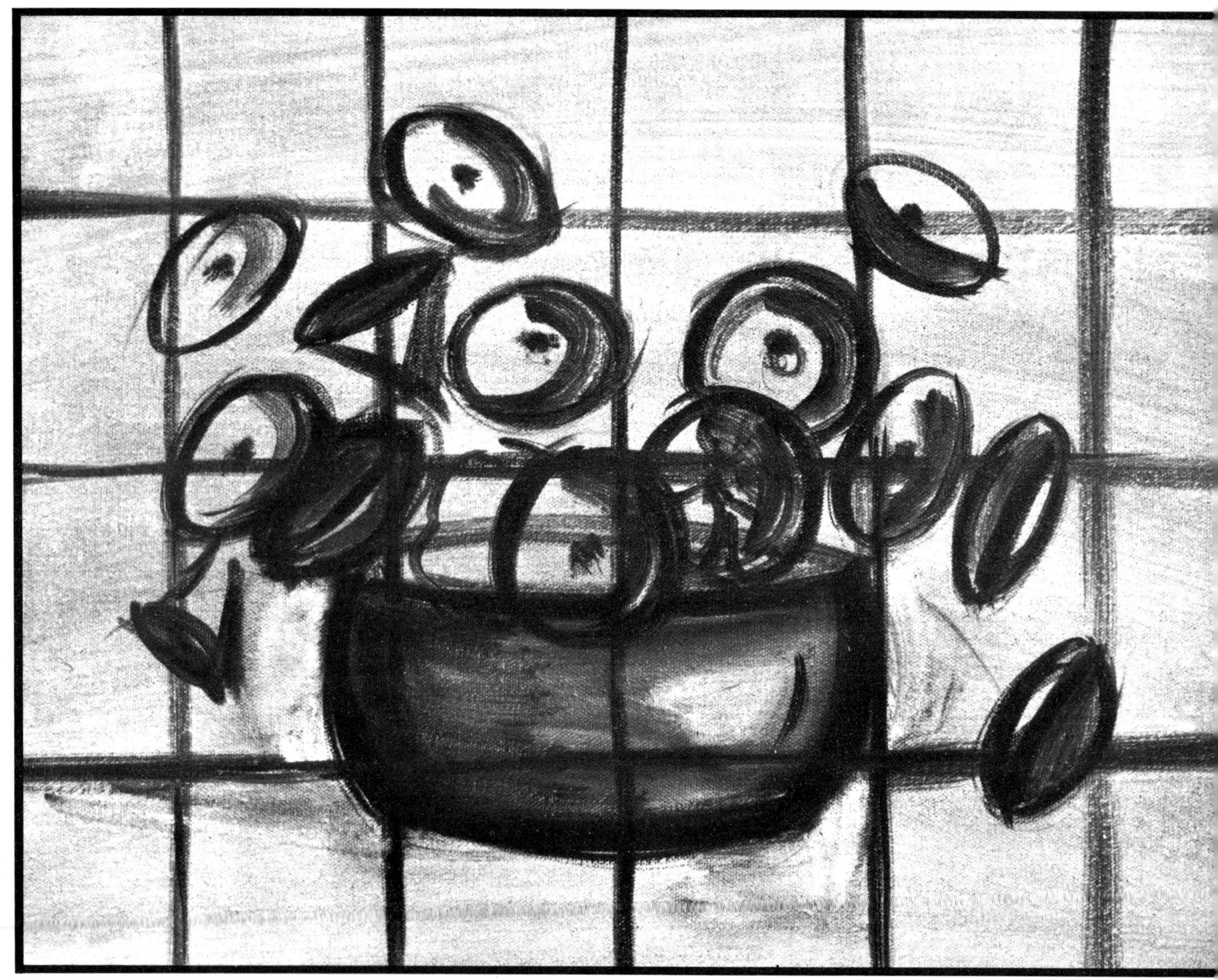

5 Paint stems in the bowl with dark, medium and light tones. Add a few touches of purple to the top of the stems.

HIGHLIGHTS AND FALLEN PETALS AND LEAVES
1 Paint a few fallen petals and leaves in the foregound with tones of red, yellow and green. Paint purple under them, for shadows.
2 Paint the highlights on the bowl with white mixed with a touch of Naples yellow.

The flowers in this painting give you an opportunity to experiment and go on your own a little.

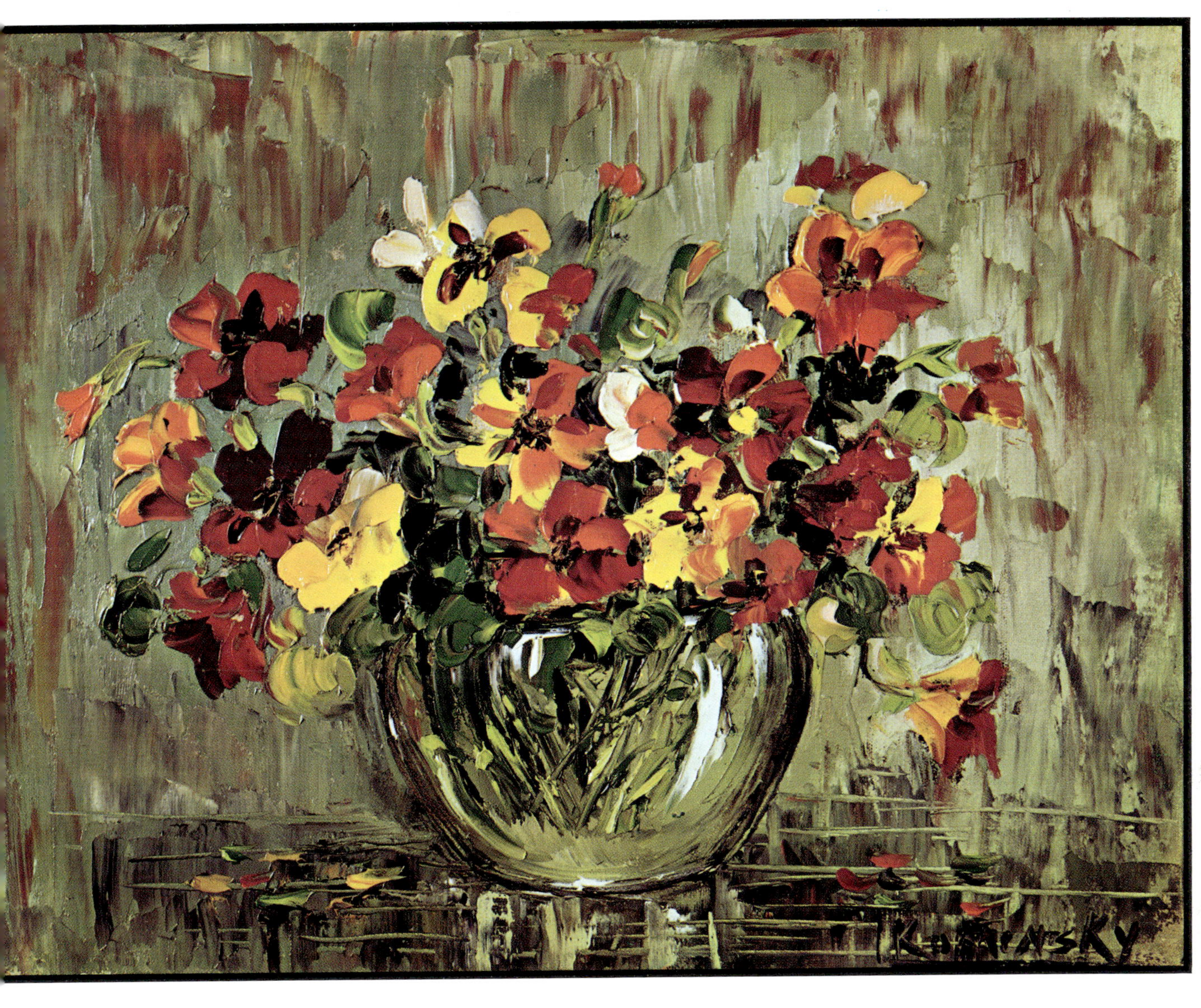

Still Life - Vegetables

THE DRAWING

1 Use canvas board, canvas or hardboard, 36cm (14 in.) by 46cm (18 in.) horizontally.
2 Study the drawing and painting on pages 38 and 39.
3 Arrange the palette according to the palette layout on page 8.
4 Use the large, flat hog brush to stain the canvas with a light wash of burnt umber, as described in Step 1 on page 7. Wipe with toilet tissue.
5 With the medium round brush and dark umber wash put in the grid lines and simple drawing as indicated on page 38. Draw the soup tureen in a square first to keep the sides even.
6 The light is coming from the left, so lightly shade the right of the tureen and vegetables.
7 Clean your brushes in the medium of turpentine or white spirit.

THE PAINTING

BACKGROUND

Colour formula
Tones of greyed dark green

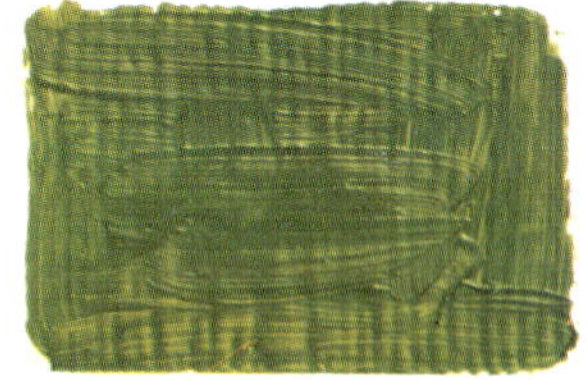  

| light | medium | dark |

Medium tone
1 tablespoon yellow ochre
$\frac{1}{2}$ teaspoon mixed green
$\frac{1}{2}$ teaspoon purple
Mix and separate into three parts, one small ($\frac{1}{2}$ teaspoon) and two equal parts.
First part ($\frac{1}{2}$ teaspoon) for light tone
add **1 tablespoon white**
$\frac{1}{8}$ teaspoon yellow ochre

Second part for medium tone: do not touch

Third part for dark tone
add **$\frac{1}{2}$ teaspoon purple**
$\frac{1}{4}$ teaspoon viridian
$\frac{1}{4}$ teaspoon yellow ochre

Clean your knife.

Let's paint
Use offset knife, held lightly.

1 Study the painting on page 39.
2 Paint dark tone on the right of the canvas, using long, downward strokes.
3 Paint medium tone in the middle and light tone on the left of the canvas.
4 Using the flat of the knife paint downward strokes of purple under objects, for shadows.

Add a little cadmium orange and vermilion, then score this area horizontally with clean knife.
5 Paint a few light strokes of cadmium orange on the left of the background and a few light strokes of purple on the right.

SOUP TUREEN

Colour formula
Tones of burnt orange

light   medium   dark

Medium tone
1 tablespoon cadmium orange
½ teaspoon vermilion
¼ teaspoon purple
Mix and separate into three parts, one small (½ teaspoon) and two equal parts.
First part (½ teaspoon) for light tone
add   ½ teaspoon white
½ teaspoon cadmium orange
¼ teaspoon cadmium yellow deep

Second part for medium tone: do not touch

Third part for dark tone
add   ¼ teaspoon purple
¼ teaspoon alizarin crimson

1 Study the soup tureen in the painting on page 39.
2 Paint the right side of the tureen with curved, flat strokes of dark tone. Leave the top for now.
3 Paint medium tone in the centre and light tone on the left. Blend lightly.
4 Paint the top of the tureen with dark tone on the right, medium tone in the middle and light tone on the left. Paint the lip in the same way, taking care to retain the curve.
5 Paint the right handle with dark tone, adding touches of medium and light tones where indicated.
6 Paint the left handle with dark tone on the inside and medium tone on the outside, adding a little light tone. Paint the knob on top with light and medium tones.
7 Mix a little purple with some dark tone and use this to outline the soup tureen. Highlights will be added later.

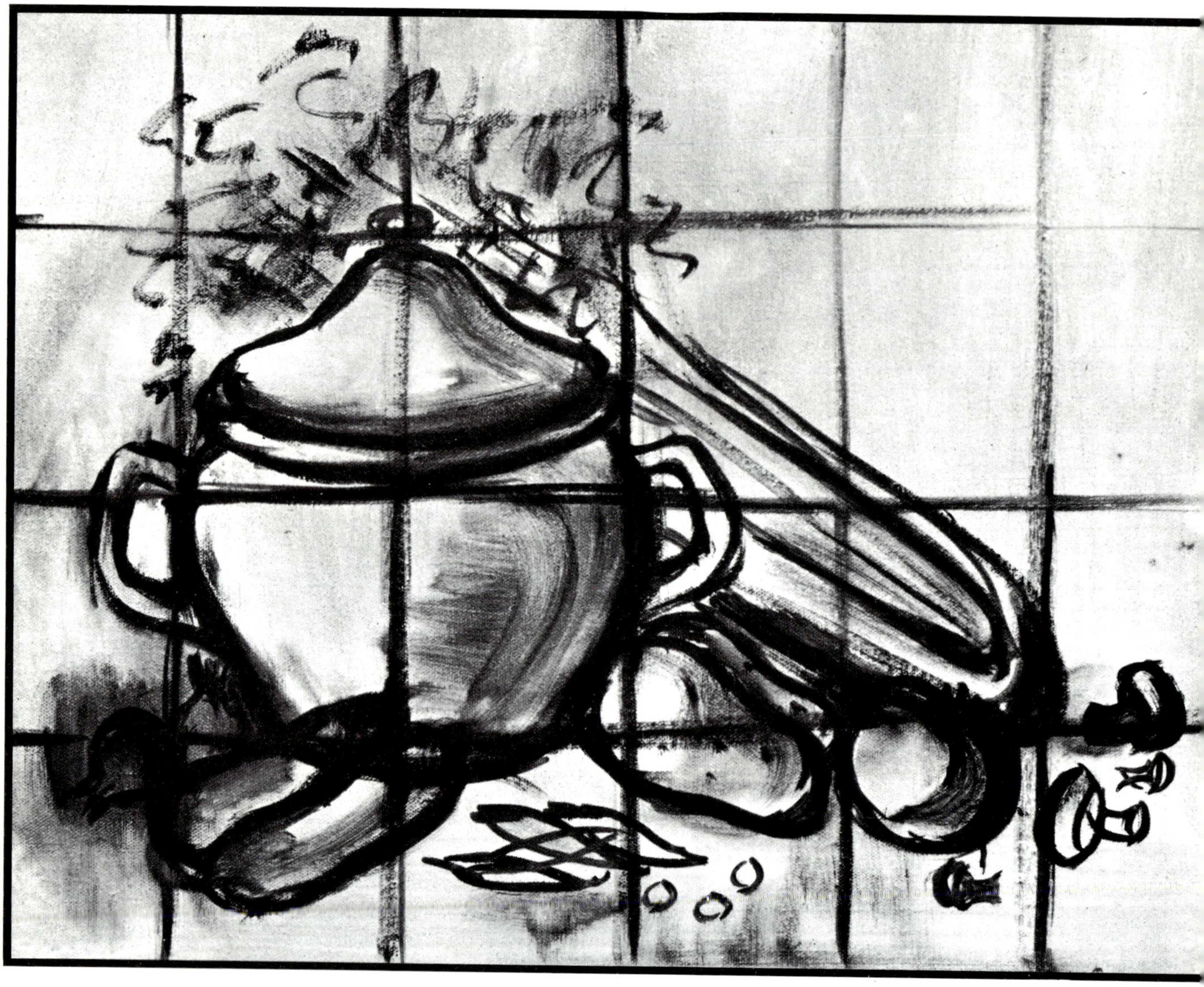

CELERY, COURGETTES AND PEAS

**Colour formula
Tones of green**

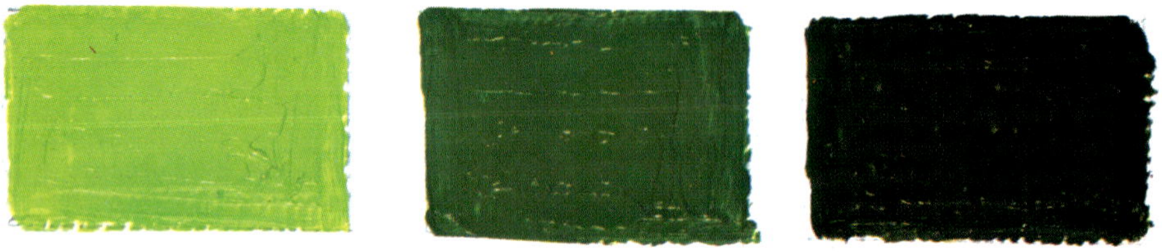

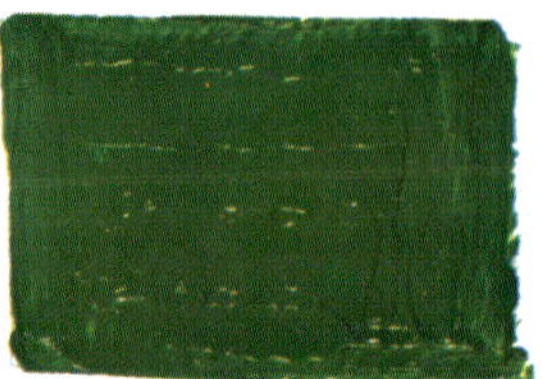

light   medium   dark

Refer to page 14 for tones of green and mix according to the directions.

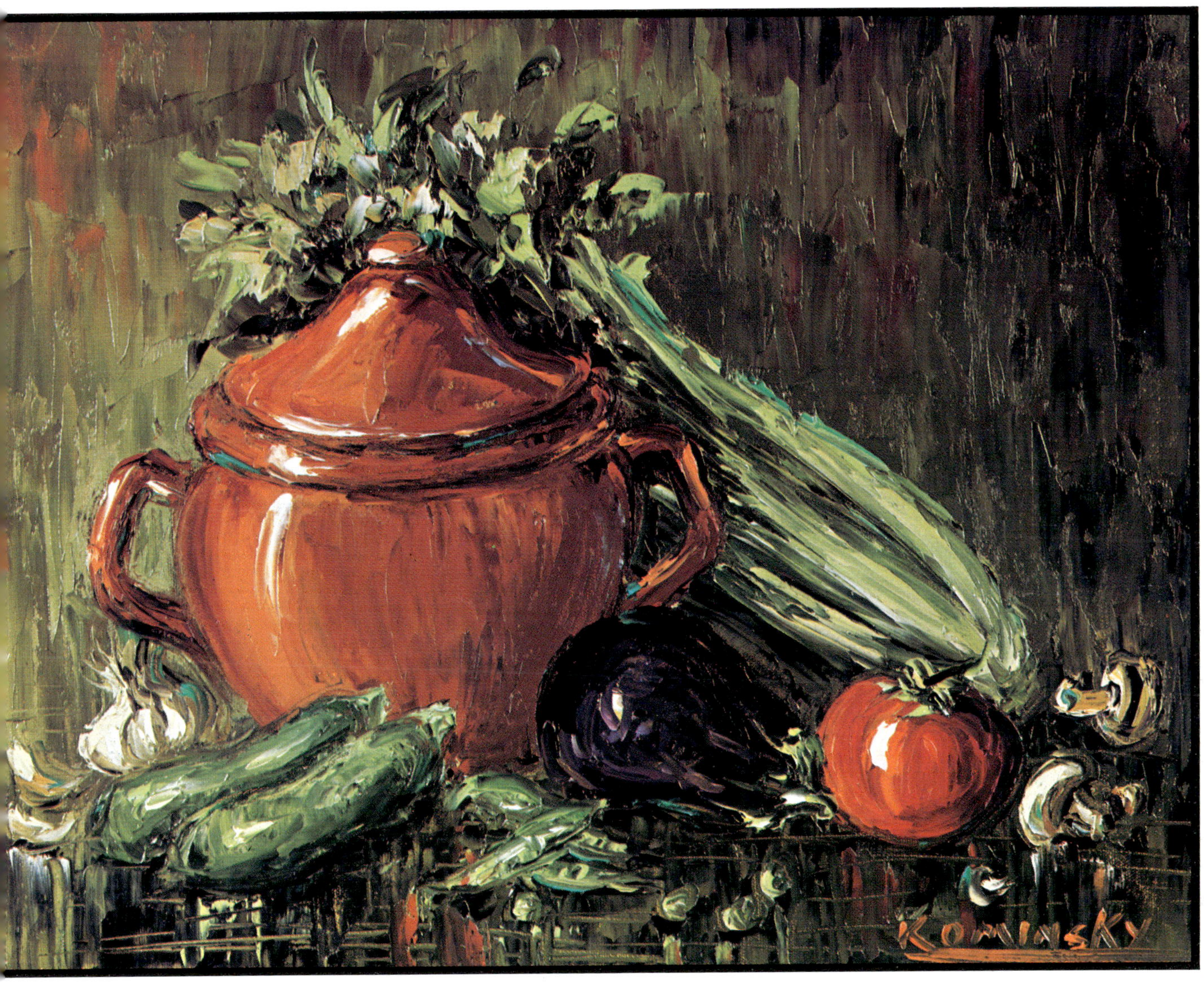

CELERY
1 Study the celery in the painting above.
2 Paint the celery stalks in shadow behind the soup tureen with dark and medium tones. Take care not to lose the handle of the tureen.
3 Paint the base of the stalks with medium and light tones. Keep the stalks separate by painting between them with dark tone and purple. Use long strokes and give the tones a rough texture. Blend stalks lightly.
4 Paint a few strokes of Naples yellow near the base of the stalks.
5 Paint the leaves directly behind the tureen with blobs of dark tone and purple. Paint the leaves above these with medium and light tones.

COURGETTES
1 Study the courgettes in the painting above.
2 Paint the right side of each courgette with dark tone.
3 Paint the centre of each with medium tone and the left side with light tone. Blend tones lightly.

4 Paint the stems with light tone.

PEAS
1 Study the peas in the painting on the previous page.
2 Paint pods with medium and light tones.
3 Paint separate peas with dark tone and edge them on the left side with light tone.

TOMATO

Colours
Tones of red

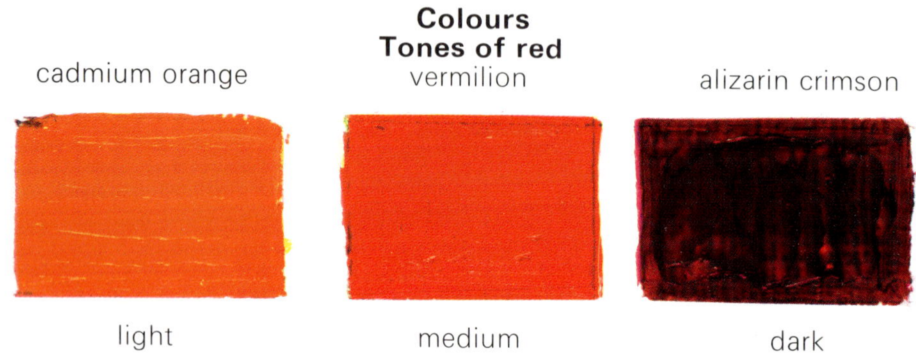

The above colours are used from the palette and require no mixing.

1 Study the tomato in the painting on the previous page.
2 Paint dark tone on the right side and bottom of the tomato, using circular strokes, then medium tone in the middle and light tone on the left. Blend tones lightly.
3 Paint the leaves and stem with a few short strokes of light and dark green tones.

AUBERGINE

Colour tones

to add
$\frac{1}{2}$ **teaspoon medium greyed dark green tone**
$\frac{1}{4}$ **teaspoon purple**

to add
$\frac{1}{2}$ **teaspoon light greyed dark green tone**
$\frac{1}{8}$ **teaspoon purple**
$\frac{1}{4}$ **teaspoon white**
touch of Naples yellow

1 Study the aubergine in the painting on the previous page.
2 Paint dark tone on the right side and bottom of the aubergine, using circular strokes.
3 Paint light tone on the rest of the aubergine, again using circular strokes.
4 Outline the whole of the aubergine with purple from palette.
5 Paint the green top with medium and light green tones.

MUSHROOMS AND GARLIC
1 Study the mushrooms and garlic in the painting on the previous page.
2 Paint the top mushroom with yellow ochre and highlight it with Naples yellow. Outline it with purple.
3 Paint the stalks of the lower mushrooms with yellow ochre and the tops with Naples yellow. Outline them with purple.
4 Paint the right side of the garlic and the two separate cloves with yellow ochre and the left side with Naples yellow. Outline the right side lightly with purple.

HIGHLIGHTS

Colour tone
$\frac{3}{4}$ teaspoon white
$\frac{1}{4}$ teaspoon Naples yellow

1 Paint highlights of the above tone carefully on soup tureen in the shape of the object.
2 Paint a blob of above tone for highlight on tomato, aubergine and courgettes.
3 Paint blobs of Naples yellow in celery leaves where indicated.
4 Paint a few touches of aqua lightly on objects where indicated.

Now you have the experience of painting different vegetables.

Yellow Tulips

THE DRAWING

1 Use canvas board, canvas or hardboard, 36cm (14 in.) by 46cm (18 in.) vertically.
2 Study the drawing and painting on pages 44 and 45.
3 Arrange the palette according to the palette layout on page 8.
4 Use the large, flat hog brush to stain the canvas with a light wash of burnt umber, as described in Step 1 on page 7. Wipe with toilet tissue.
5 With the medium round brush and dark umber wash put in the grid lines and simple drawing as indicated on page 44. Note the position of the flowers and make sure they go into the vase.
6 The light is coming from the right, so with dark umber wash lightly shade the left side of the tulips and vase.
7 Clean your brushes in the medium of turpentine or white spirit.

THE PAINTING

BACKGROUND

Colour formula
Tones of greyed light green

light   medium   dark

Refer to page 21 for tones of greyed light green and mix according to the directions.

Clean your knife.

Let's paint
Use offset knife, held lightly.

1 Study the background in the painting on page 45.
2 Paint the background in thirds of light, medium and dark tones, starting on the left with dark tone. Blend tones lightly and go around flowers loosely.
3 With flat of knife lightly paint strokes of purple and aqua into the background.
4 Paint downward strokes of purple under the vase, for shadows. Add a few touches of aqua, then with clean knife score the shadows horizontally, for reflections.

VASE

**Colour formula
Tones of blue**

light   medium   dark

Refer to page 16 for tones of blue and mix according to the directions.

1 Study the vase in the painting on page 45.
2 Paint dark tone at the top of the vase and shading down on each side. Paint the raised bottom with the same dark tone.
3 Paint a little medium tone in the centre of the vase and light tone over the rim of the raised bottom. Blend tones lightly.
4 Paint blue from palette over dark tone on the sides and across the bottom of the vase. Blend lightly.
5 Paint touches of aqua over light tone, for brilliance.
6 Outline the left side and bottom of vase with purple. Highlights will be added later.

TULIPS

**Colours
Tones of yellow**

Naples yellow   lemon yellow   cadmium yellow deep   yellow ochre

light   medium   dark   extra dark

The above colours are used from the palette and require no mixing.

1 Study the tulips in the painting on page 45.
2 Paint the flowers on the left half of the bunch with extra dark tone on the left of the flowers, then dark and medium tones. Paint light tone on the right side of these flowers. Create petals with strokes.
3 Paint light tone at the base of the two drooping flowers on the left.
4 Paint the flowers on the right half with light tone at the top. Paint the front petals with medium and dark tones, adding extra dark tone at the base of the flowers. Blend tones slightly.

43

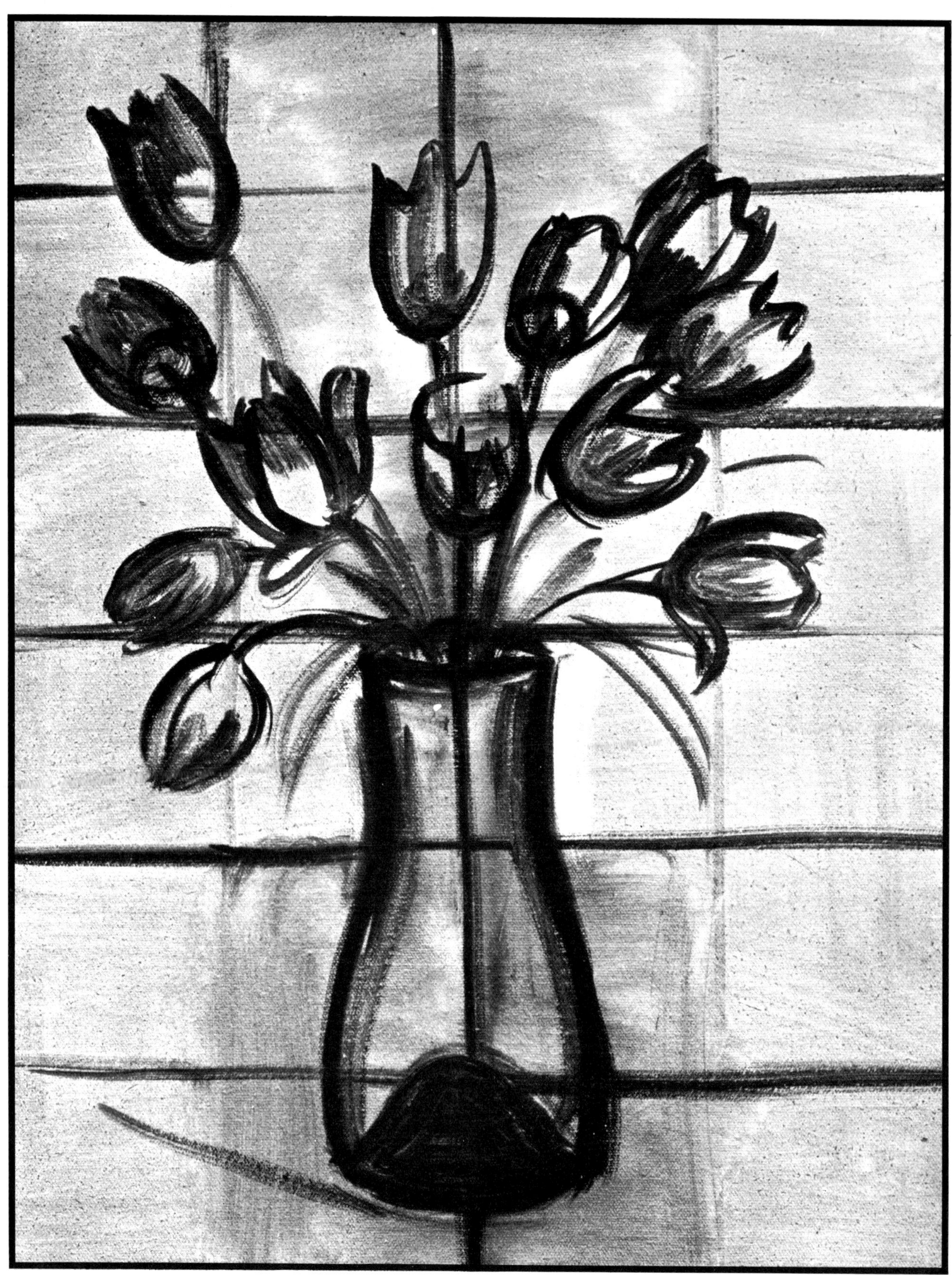

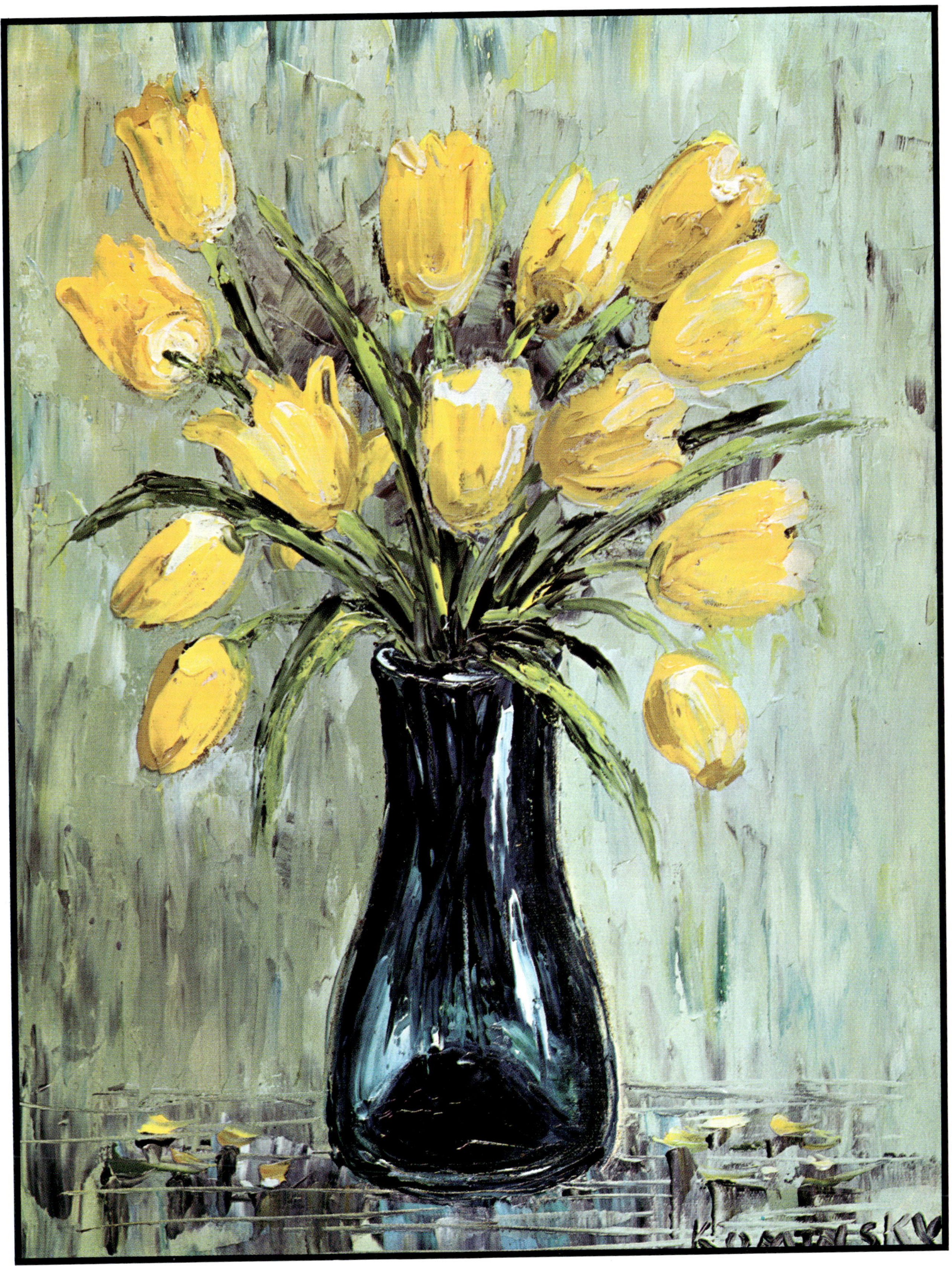

LEAVES AND STEMS

**Colour formula
Tones of green**

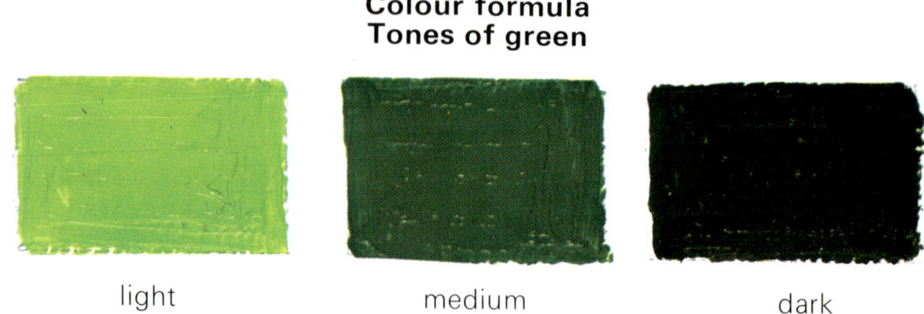

lightmediumdark

Refer to page 14 for tones of green and mix according to the directions.

1 Study the leaves and stems in the painting on the previous page. They are exposed and distinctive in shape.
2 Paint the top of the rather thick stems with light tone, shading to medium and dark tones.
3 Paint strokes of purple on these stems going into the vase, then add a few touches of purple between the flowers.
4 Paint the spiky leaves with dark tone on the top, blending in medium and light tones.
5 Paint a few fallen petals with medium and light yellow tones. Paint purple under these petals, for shadows.

The lovely vase in this painting is an unusual shape and colour.

San Juan Mountains, Colorado

THE DRAWING

1 Use canvas board, canvas or hardboard, 36cm (14 in.) by 46cm (18 in.) horizontally.
2 Study the drawing and painting on pages 48 and 49.
3 Arrange the palette according to the palette layout on page 8.
4 Use the large, flat hog brush to stain the canvas with a light wash of burnt umber, as described in Step 1 on page 7. Wipe with toilet tissue.
5 With the medium round brush and dark umber wash put in the grid lines and simple drawing as indicated on page 48.
6 The light is coming from the left, so with dark umber wash lightly shade the areas where indicated.
7 Clean your brushes in the medium of turpentine or white spirit.

THE PAINTING

SKY

**Colour formula
Sky tones**

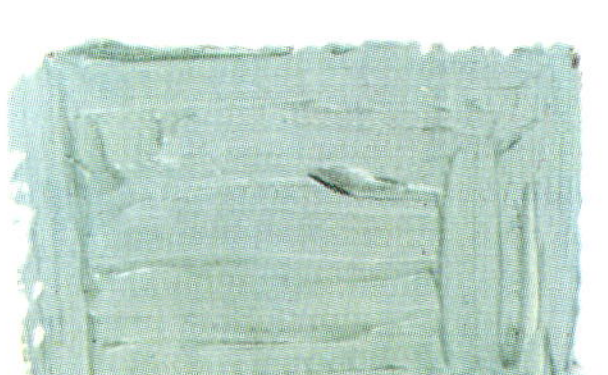  

| light | medium | dark |

Refer to page 26 for sky tones and mix according to the directions.
In this painting only the light and medium tones are used for the sky. The dark tone is used for the mountains.

Clean your knife.

Let's paint
Use offset knife, held lightly.

1 Study the sky in the painting on page 49.
2 Paint light tone around the tops of the mountains and up into the sky. (Use flat of the knife as the point makes ridges.)
3 Paint the remaining sky area with medium tone, dragging the colour from the top of the canvas down to the mountains in slanting strokes. Blend the tones but take care to retain the light tone around the mountains.

MOUNTAINS

**Colour tones
to   each of the medium and dark sky tones
add   ⅛ teaspoon purple**

1 Study the mountains in the painting on page 49.
2 Paint the right side of the mountains with dark tone and the left side with medium tone. Use long, flowing strokes.

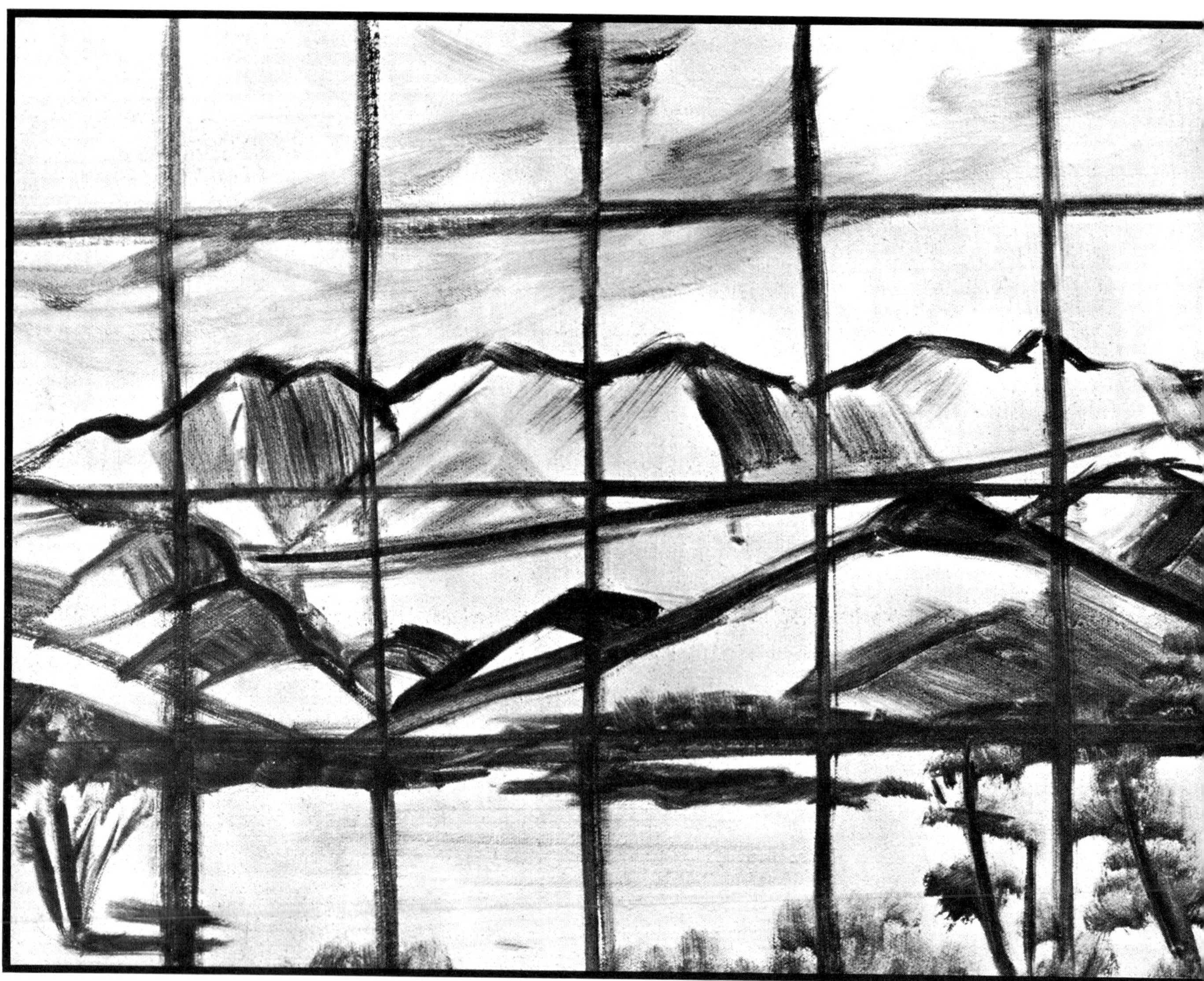

3 Clean knife, then lightly and carefully drag a bit of sky into the mountains to soften the
line. Take care not to lose the mountains.

SNOW

Colour tone
1 tablespoon white
$\frac{1}{8}$ teaspoon Naples yellow

1 Study the snow on the mountains in the painting opposite.
2 Paint the left side of the mountains with the above tone. Skim the surface of the
mountains in a long, sweeping stroke.

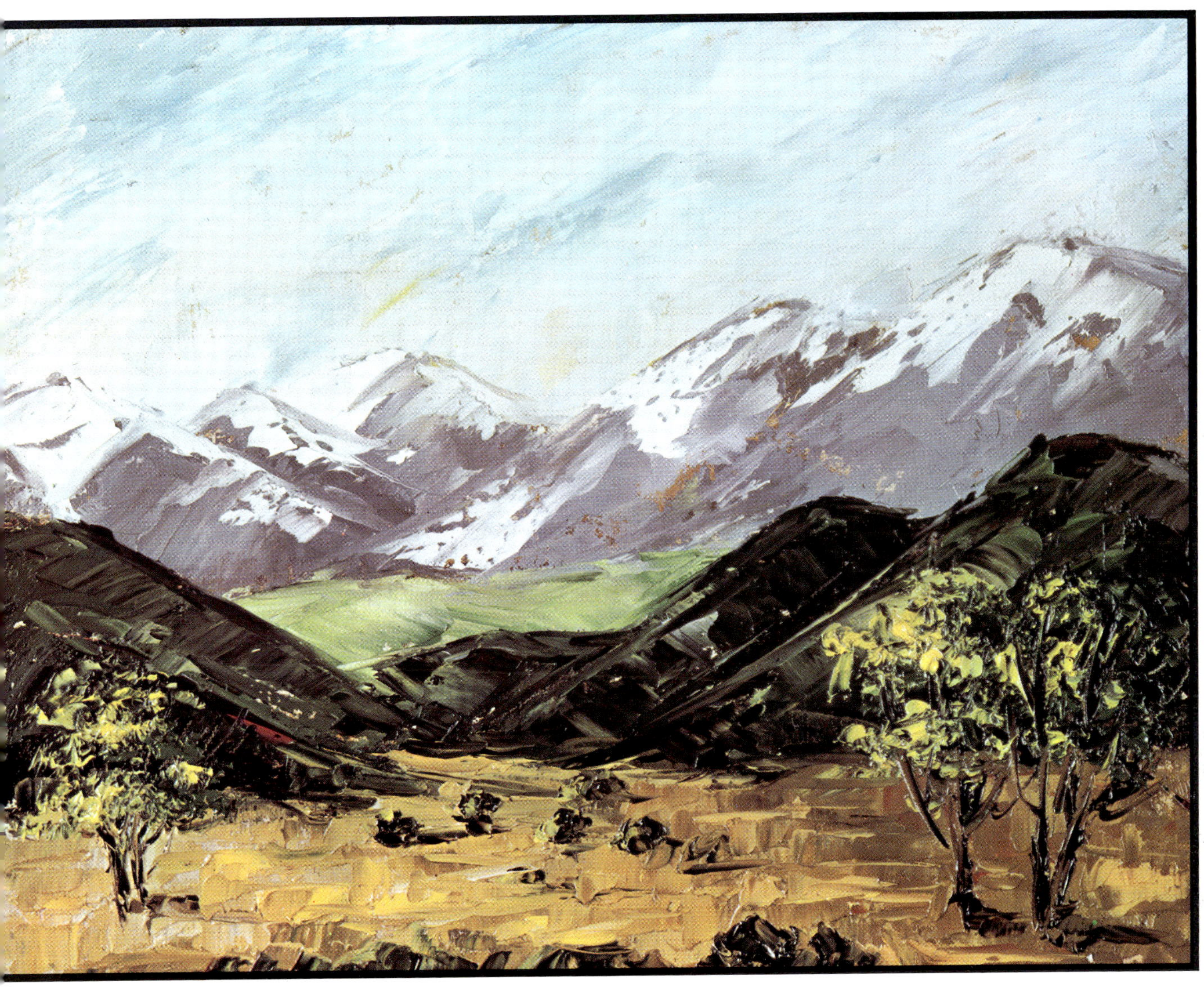

GREEN HILLS

**Colour formula
Tones of green**

| light | medium | dark |

Refer to page 14 for tones of green and mix according to the directions. You will need an additional tone for the pale area at the base of the mountains, which you mix in the following way:

Extra light tone
to   half the original light green tone
add   ½ teaspoon white
touch of purple

1   Study the green hills in the painting on the previous page.
2   Paint the hill at the base of the mountains with extra light tone. Keep the area small.
3   Paint the dark hills with dark tone, using long, flowing strokes.
4   Paint purple into the dark tone on the right side and at the base of all hills. Blend tones slightly and keep the base of the hills uneven.
5   Keep left-over tones of green for the trees and bushes which will be painted later.

YELLOW GRASS

Colour formula
Tones of yellow ochre

light   medium   dark

Refer to page 17 for tones of yellow ochre and mix according to the directions.

1   Study the yellow grass in the painting on the previous page.
2   With the flat of the knife paint short, downward strokes of dark tone on the right side and along bottom of canvas. Keep your strokes uneven and textured.
3   Paint medium tone next working towards and into the green hills. Blend slightly.
4   Paint light tone on the left of the canvas, blending the tones.

TREES AND BUSHES

For these you will need the tones of green previously mixed for the hills.

1   Study the trees and bushes in the painting on the previous page.
2   Paint the small tree trunks on the left with purple. Keep them slender.
3   Paint the trunks of the larger trees on the right with purple.
4   Paint the foliage across the trees by stippling medium green tone on the right and light tone on the left. Do not make the foliage solid.
5   Paint the small round bushes with dark tone on the right side and light tone on the left side.
6   Paint scrub in the foreground with dark and medium tones, adding a touch of vermilion.
7   Drag a bit of purple along right side of bushes and trees, for shadows.

This painting is relaxing to look at and paint.

White Daisies

THE DRAWING

1 Use canvas board, canvas or hardboard, 36cm (14 in.) by 46cm (18 in.) vertically.
2 Study the drawing and painting on pages 52 and 53.
3 Arrange the palette according to the palette layout on page 8.
4 Use the large, flat hog brush to stain the canvas with a light wash of burnt umber, as described in Step 1 on page 7. Wipe with toilet tissue.
5 With the medium round brush and dark umber wash put in the grid lines and simple drawing as indicated on page 52. Note position of daisies.
6 The light is coming from the right, so with dark umber wash lightly shade in areas where indicated.
7 Clean your brushes in the medium of turpentine or white spirit.

THE PAINTING

BACKGROUND

**Colour formula
Tones of yellow ochre**

light   medium   dark

Refer to page 17 for tones of yellow ochre and mix according to the directions.

Clean your knife.

Let's paint
Use offset knife, held lightly.

1 Study the background in the painting on page 53.
2 Paint dark tone on the left of the canvas, using long, downward strokes. Go between flowers loosely.
3 Paint medium tone in the middle and light tone on the right of the canvas.
4 Using the flat of the knife paint downward strokes of purple under vase, for shadows. Add a little cadmium orange, then score this area horizontally with clean knife, for reflections.
5 Paint a few strokes of purple and cadmium orange in the background where indicated.

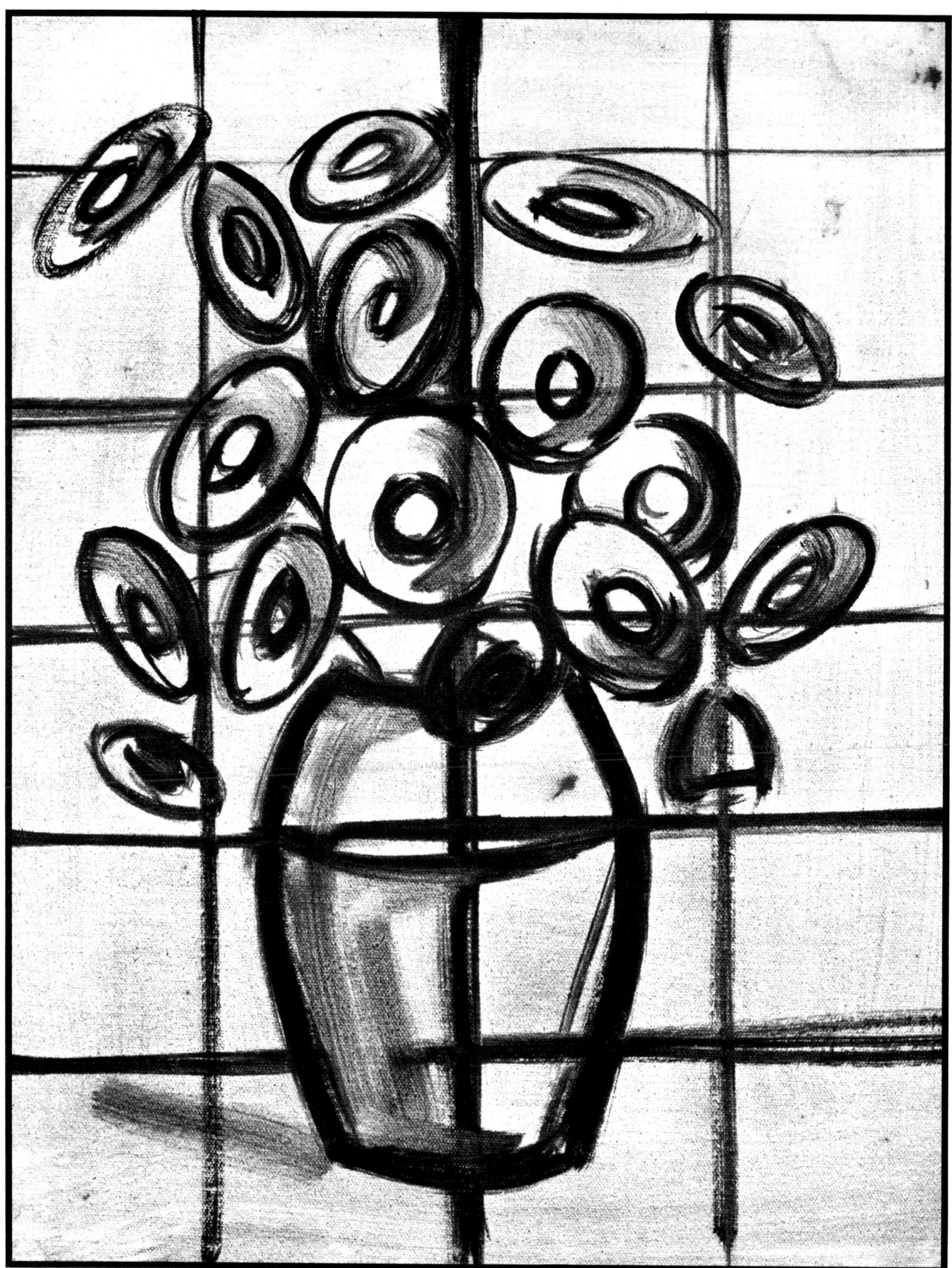

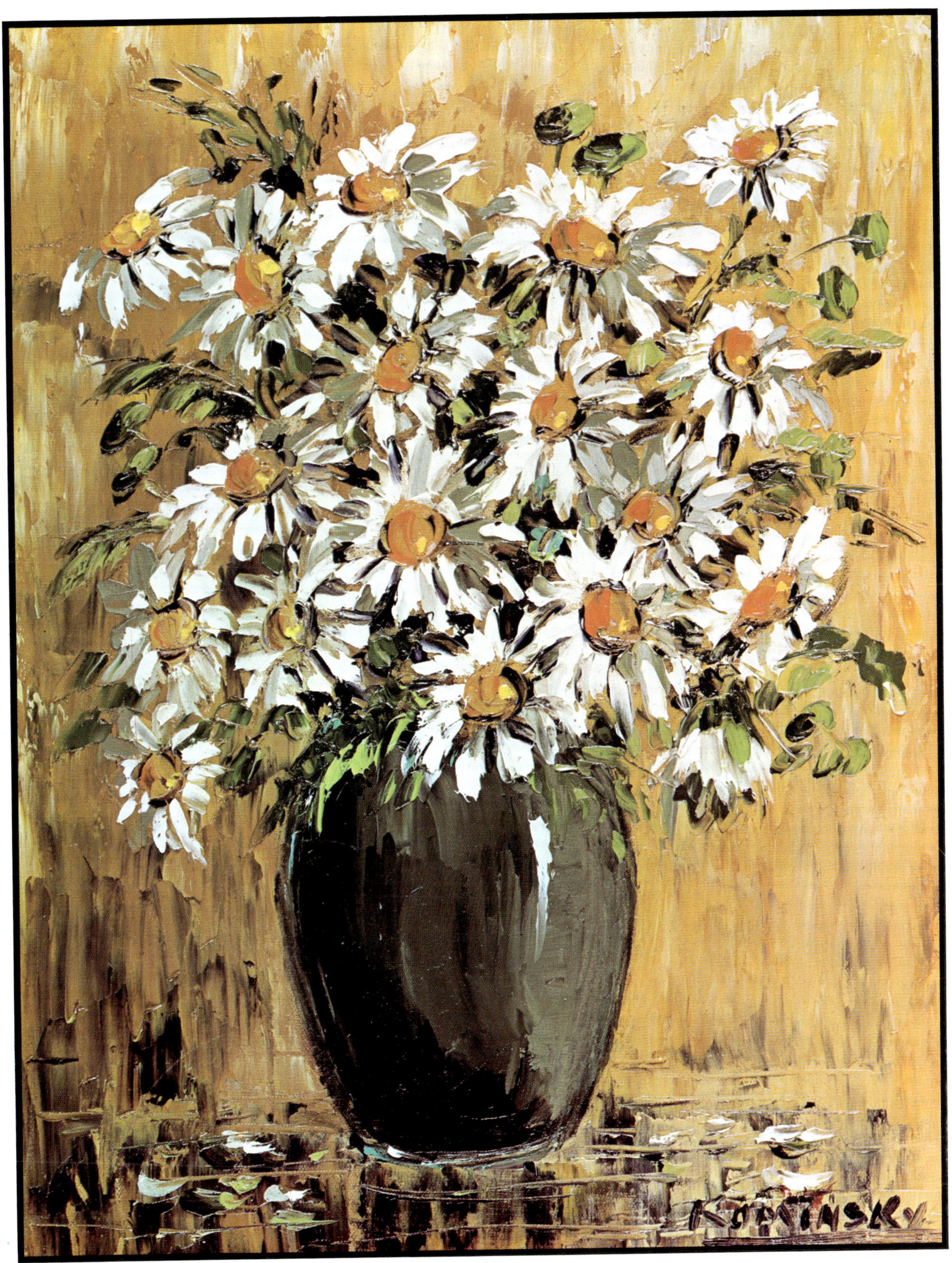

Korinsky

VASE

**Colour formula
Tones of black**

light   medium   dark

The procedure for mixing this colour is different from previous methods.

**Dark tone
$\frac{3}{4}$ tablespoon burnt umber
$\frac{3}{4}$ tablespoon blue**

Mix and separate into three parts, one small ($\frac{1}{2}$ teaspoon) for light tone and two
equal parts.

First part for dark tone: do not touch

**Second part for medium tone
add $\frac{3}{4}$ teaspoon white
$\frac{1}{8}$ teaspoon yellow ochre
touch of aqua**

**Third part ($\frac{1}{2}$ teaspoon) for light tone
add 1 teaspoon white
$\frac{1}{8}$ teaspoon yellow ochre
touch of aqua**

1 Study the vase in the painting on the previous page.
2 Paint dark tone on the left side and bottom of vase, using long, flat strokes.
3 Paint medium tone in the middle and light tone on the right side. Blend slightly but
   do not lose tonal values. The highlight will be added later.

DAISIES

**Colour formula
Tones of white**

 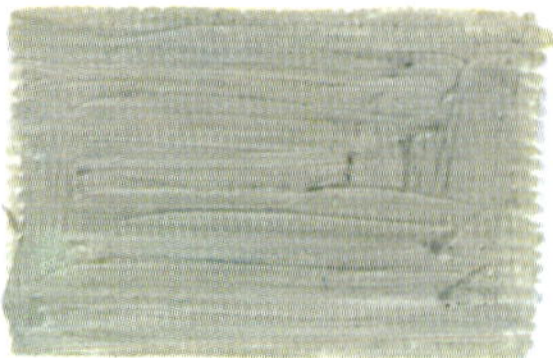 

light   medium   dark

Refer to page 10 for tones of white and mix according to the directions.

1 Study the daisies in the painting on the previous page.
2 Paint the petals on the right half of each daisy with medium and dark tones.
3 Paint the petals on the left half of each daisy with light tone.

54

4 Paint the tips of the dark petals with light tone, catching the light.
5 Paint the tips of the light petals with dark tone, in shadow. Do not curve the petals.

CENTRES
1 Study the centres of the flowers in the painting on page 53.
2 Paint the centres with yellow ochre, dragging the colour slightly into the petals.
3 Paint a spot of cadmium orange on the left of each centre and a highlight of lemon
   yellow on the right of each centre.
4 Paint a delicate line of purple around the right side of the centres and between the
   petals where indicated, for depth.

LEAVES AND BUDS

**Colour formula
Tones of green**

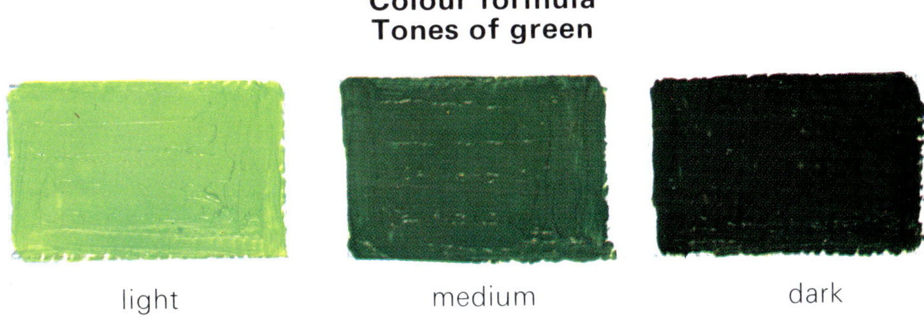

light   medium   dark

Refer to page 14 for tones of green and mix according to the directions.

1 Study the leaves and buds in the painting on page 53.
2 Paint a few leaves in between the flowers with dark and medium tones.
3 Paint an impression of leaves on the left side with dark and medium tones. Add touches
   of light tone. Keep the leaves lacy.
4 Paint a few leaves on the right side with dark, medium and light tones.
5 Paint small round buds with dark tone, adding light tone for highlights.

HIGHLIGHTS AND FALLEN PETALS AND LEAVES

**Colour tone
½ teaspoon white
⅛ teaspoon Naples yellow**

1 Paint highlights of the above tone on vase.
2 Paint in a few fallen leaves and petals using the above tone, light white tone and
   light green tone. Paint a little purple under them, for shadows.
3 Add a few touches of aqua where indicated.

This painting is not so demanding and daisies are charming.

Old Rome

THE DRAWING

1 Use canvas board, canvas or hardboard, 36cm (14 in.) by 46cm (18 in.) horizontally.
2 Study the drawing and painting on pages 58 and 59.
3 Arrange the palette according to the palette layout on page 8.
4 Use the large, flat hog brush to stain the canvas with a light wash of burnt umber, as described in Step 1 on page 7. Wipe with toilet tissue.
5 With the medium round brush and dark umber wash put in the grid lines and simple drawing as indicated on page 58. Study carefully the perspective of the passage. There are three doorways in it: the large entrance, the second with arch and the third small doorway at the end of the passage on the right. After these have been drawn, draw connecting lines in the four corners as indicated, for correct perspective.
6 The light is coming from the right, so with dark umber wash lightly shade in areas where indicated.
7 Clean your brushes in the medium of turpentine or white spirit.

THE PAINTING

THE PASSAGE

Colour formula
Tones of beige

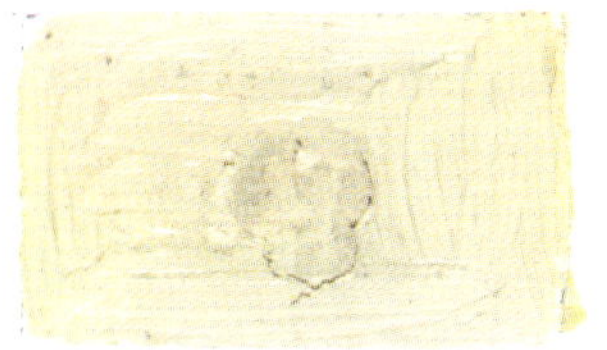   

| extra light | light | medium | dark |

You will need to mix a double batch of colour, in the following way:

Medium tone
2 tablespoons yellow ochre
1 teaspoon white
½ teaspoon lemon yellow
1 teaspoon cadmium orange
touch of purple

Mix and separate into three parts, one small (1 teaspoon) and two equal parts.

First part (1 teaspoon) for light tone
add   **¾ tablespoon white**
      ½ teaspoon Naples yellow
      ½ teaspoon cadmium orange

Second part for medium tone: do not touch

Third part for dark tone
add   **¾ teaspoon purple**
      ½ teaspoon cadmium orange
      touch of green

Clean your knife.

Let's paint
Use offset knife, held lightly.

1 Study the passage in the painting on page 59.
2 Begin with the smallest doorway at the end of the passage. Paint it with dark tone, then outline it with purple, dragging a little downwards with the flat of the knife. Add a few touches of light tone.
3 Paint the area directly around it with dark tone. Paint the ray of light with light tone. The blue tones will be added later.
4 Paint the arched doorway with dark tone, the square first, then round off the arch with purple. Blend tones.
5 Paint the ceiling of the passage with dark and medium tones. Blend a few strokes of purple on the right side, as indicated.
6 Paint the right wall of the passage with dark tone and purple. Take care not to lose the perspective in the drawing. Outline the edges of the ceiling with purple.
7 Paint the ray of light on the left wall of the passage and the floor with light tone. Paint the remaining area on the left wall with dark tone.
8 Paint the remaining area of the floor with medium and dark tones, using horizontal strokes. Paint a few purple strokes on the right side and drag a little purple into the light area on the left.
9 Paint the entire outside frame of the doorway with light tone, adding purple where indicated.

BLUE DOORWAY

Colour tones

to $\frac{3}{4}$ **teaspoon dark tone**
add $\frac{1}{2}$ **teaspoon aqua**
       touch of blue

to $\frac{1}{2}$ **teaspoon of above tone**
add $\frac{1}{2}$ **teaspoon white**
       $\frac{1}{4}$ **teaspoon aqua**

1 Study the blue doorway in the painting on page 59.
2 Paint the left frame of the doorway with light beige tone.
3 Paint the right frame with dark beige tone and purple.
4 Paint the grill at the top with light blue tone and outline it with purple. Score paint with point of knife for grill.
5 Outline the doors with purple to retain shape.
6 Paint the right door with light tone and paint the shadow at the top with dark tone.
7 Paint the left door with light tone and the slanting shadow with dark tone.
8 Paint the step with light beige tone and add a touch of medium beige tone along the bottom of the door.
9 Paint touches of light blue tone under the ray of light at the back of the passage and down the lefthand edge of the small door.
10 Paint a few horizontal strokes of light blue tone on the floor of the passage.
11 Paint a few strokes of light blue tone on the ceiling of the passage.

WALL
1 Study the strokes and colour tones in the wall in the painting on page 59.
2 Paint the entire wall (with the exception of the hanging washing and brick areas) alternately with light, medium and dark beige tones. Using the flat of knife stroke the colour across, then down. Blend slightly but retain tones.

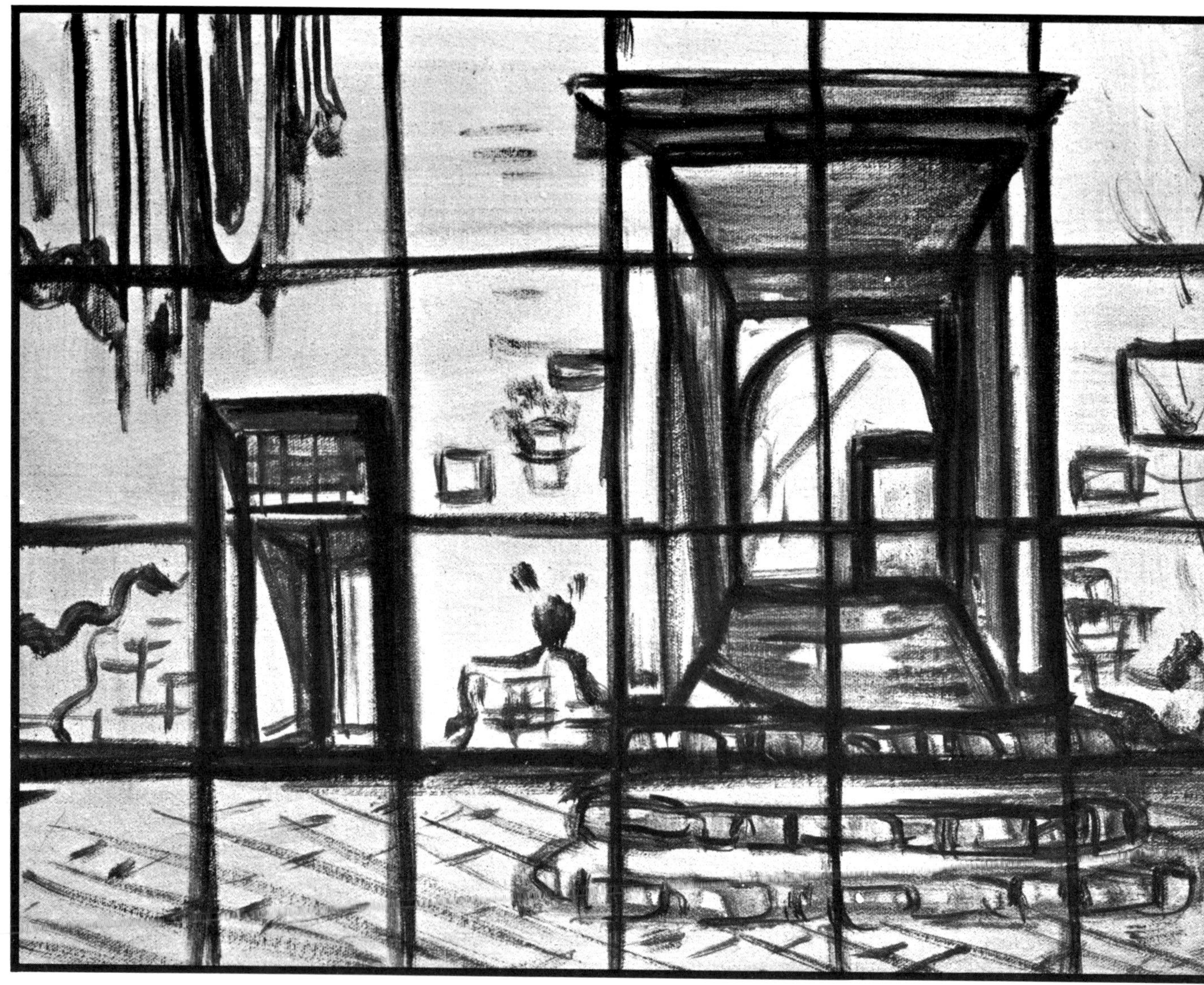

BRICK AREAS

Colour tones
to add $\frac{3}{4}$ teaspoon medium beige tone
$\frac{1}{4}$ teaspoon vermilion
touch of cadmium orange

to add $\frac{1}{2}$ teaspoon of above tone
$\frac{1}{2}$ teaspoon Naples yellow
touch of vermilion
touch of cadmium orange

1 Study the bricks in the painting opposite.
2 Paint bricks alternately with light and dark tones. Do not be precise.
3 Outline each brick area with purple, then add a few strokes of purple in between the bricks. Blend loosely.

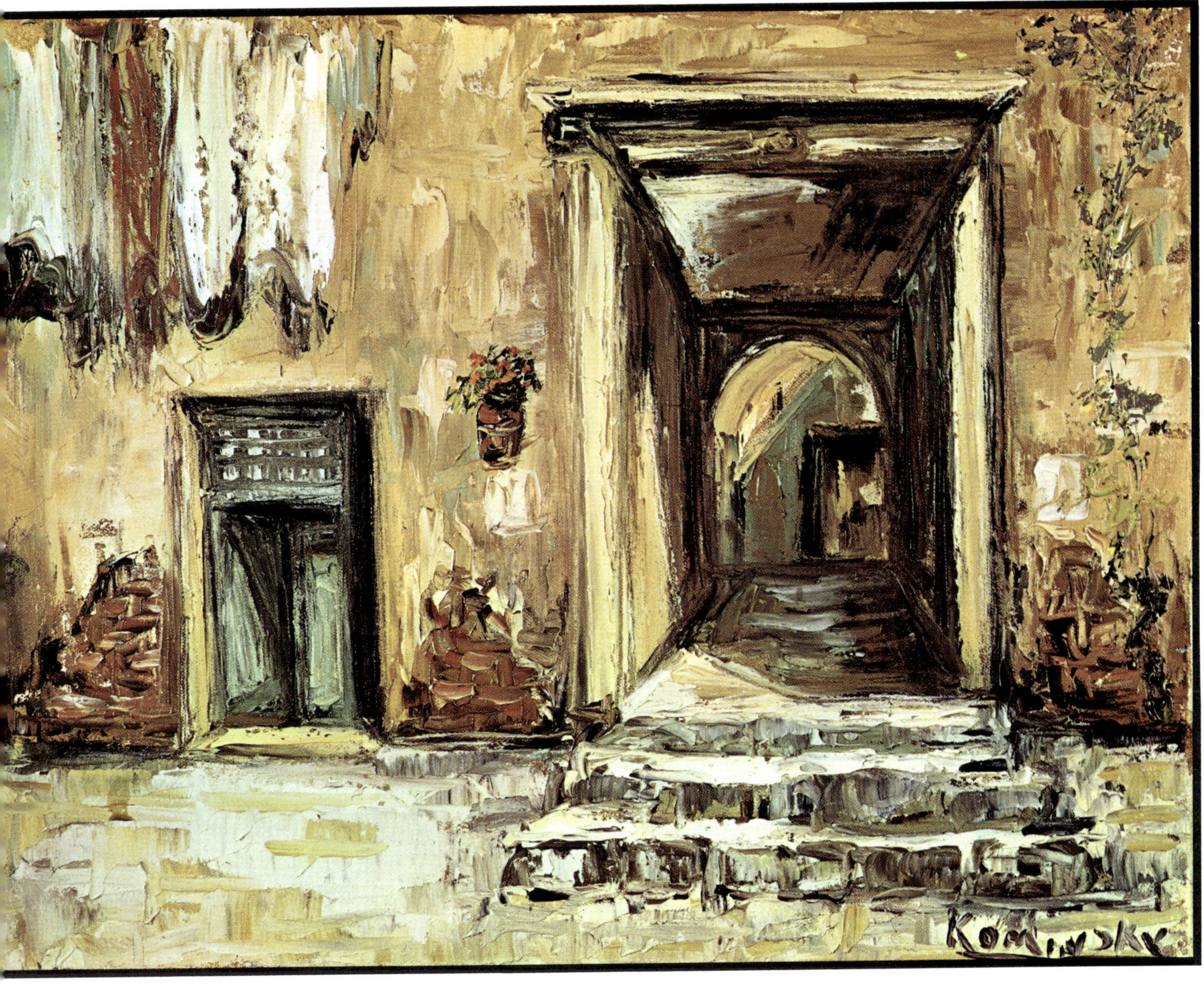

STREET AND STEPS

Colour tone
to   **remaining light beige tone**
add $\frac{1}{8}$ **teaspoon aqua**

1 Study the street and steps in the painting above. Again strokes are across and down
— notice the downward strokes on the steps.
2 Paint the entire street and the top of the steps with the above tone. Paint touches of
medium beige tone here and there.
3 For the front of the steps mix a bit of medium beige tone with purple and paint in
loosely with downward strokes, as indicated. Paint an uneven line of purple along
the bottom of the wall.

WASHING

1 Study the washing in the painting above.

2 Paint long, loose strokes of aqua and tones used for the bricks and street. Add a few touches of white.
3 Paint underneath the washing with purple, for shadows.

GERANIUMS AND VINE
1 Study the geraniums and vine in the painting on the previous page.
2 Paint the geranium pot with tones used for the bricks.
3 Paint the geranium leaves with mixed green and the flowers with cadmium orange and vermilion.
4 Mix a little lemon with mixed green to make a light green tone. Use this tone and mixed green to paint the vine on the right of the passage.
5 Add a few touches of this light green tone to the geranium leaves.

This was an ambitious project — but after all, Rome wasn't built in a day!

Wind on the Adriatic

THE DRAWING
1 Use canvas board, canvas or hardboard, 36cm (14 in.) by 46cm (18 in.) horizontally.
2 Study the drawing and painting on pages 62 and 63.
3 Arrange the palette according to the palette layout on page 8.
4 Use the large, flat hog brush to stain the canvas with a light wash of burnt umber, as described in Step 1 on page 7. Wipe with toilet tissue.
5 With the medium round brush and dark umber wash put in the grid lines and simple drawing as indicated on page 62. Don't bother about the foliage on the trees for now.
6 The light is coming from the left, so with dark umber wash lightly shade the right side of the painting where indicated.
7 Clean your brushes in the medium of turpentine or white spirit.

THE PAINTING

SKY

**Colour formula
Sky tones**

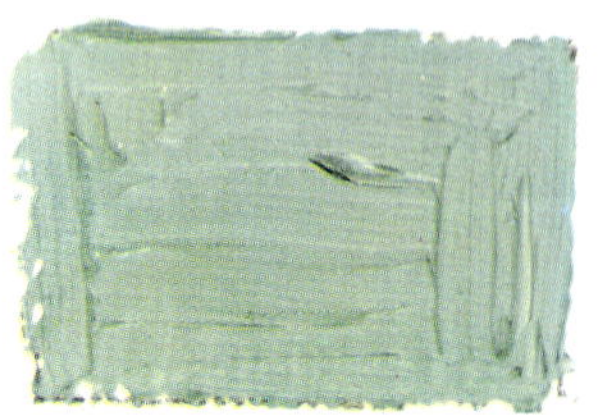  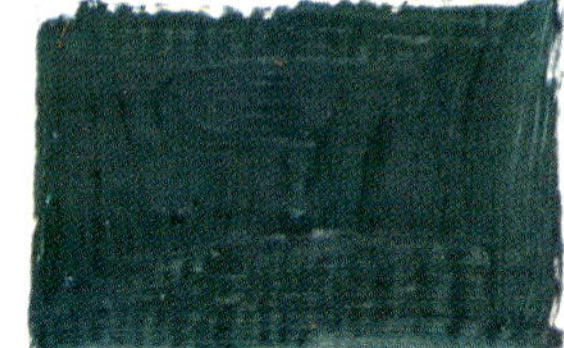

light   medium   dark

Refer to page 26 for sky tones and mix according to the directions. In this painting only the light and dark tones are used for the sky. The medium tone is used for the sea. You will need an additional tone for the sky which you mix in the following way:

Extra dark tone

to   **half the dark sky tone**
add $\frac{1}{2}$ **teaspoon mixed green**
     $\frac{1}{4}$ **teaspoon purple**
     $\frac{1}{4}$ **teaspoon cadmium orange**

Let's paint
Use offset knife, held lightly.

1 Study the dramatic sky in the painting on page 63.
2 Paint horizontal strokes of light sky tone along the horizon and a third of the way into the sky.
3 Paint this same light tone in the middle of the sky, between the two cloud banks.
4 Paint the cloud bank at the top of the canvas with dark tone, then paint extra dark tone along the bottom of this cloud bank. Use the flat of knife in half-rounded strokes. Take care not to lose the light tone in the middle of the sky.
5 Paint the cloud bank in the middle of the sky in the same way. Create a feeling of movement with your strokes. Do not lose the light tone on the water line.

SEA

Colour tone

to	**remaining extra dark tone**
add	**$\frac{1}{8}$ teaspoon viridian**
	$\frac{1}{8}$ teaspoon blue
	touch of purple
	touch of cadmium orange

1 Study the sea in the painting on page 63.
2 Paint along the entire water line with the above tone, blending it slightly with the sky.
3 Paint the rest of the sea with medium and light sky tones.
4 Paint the white horses with white mixed with a touch of Naples yellow.

FOREGROUND
Tones of green and tones of yellow are used alternately in the foreground.

**Colour formula
Tones of green**

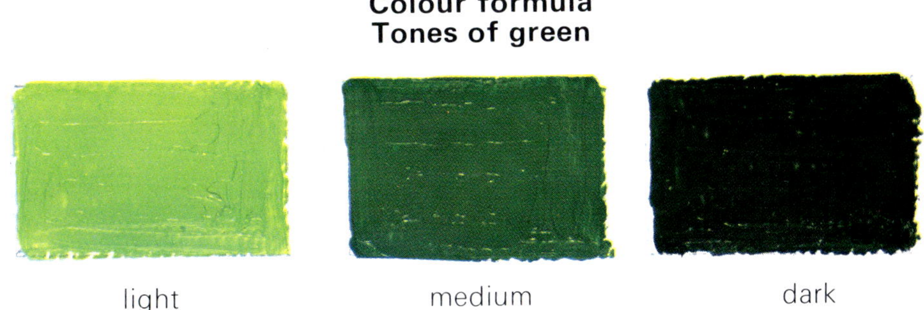

light   medium   dark

Refer to page 14 for tones of green and mix according to the directions.

**Colour formula
Tones of yellow ochre**

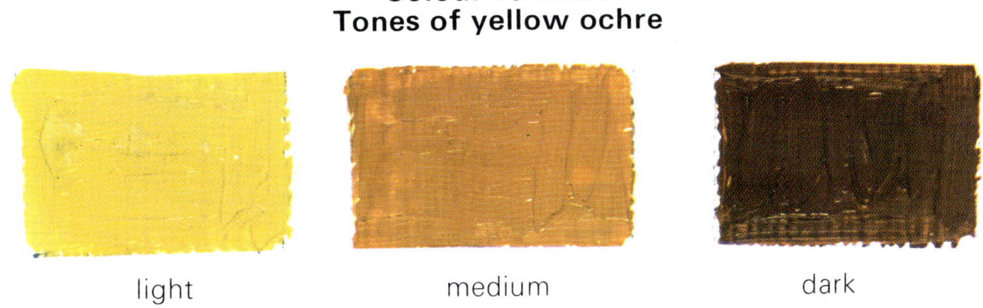

light   medium   dark

Refer to page 17 for tones of yellow ochre and mix according to the directions.

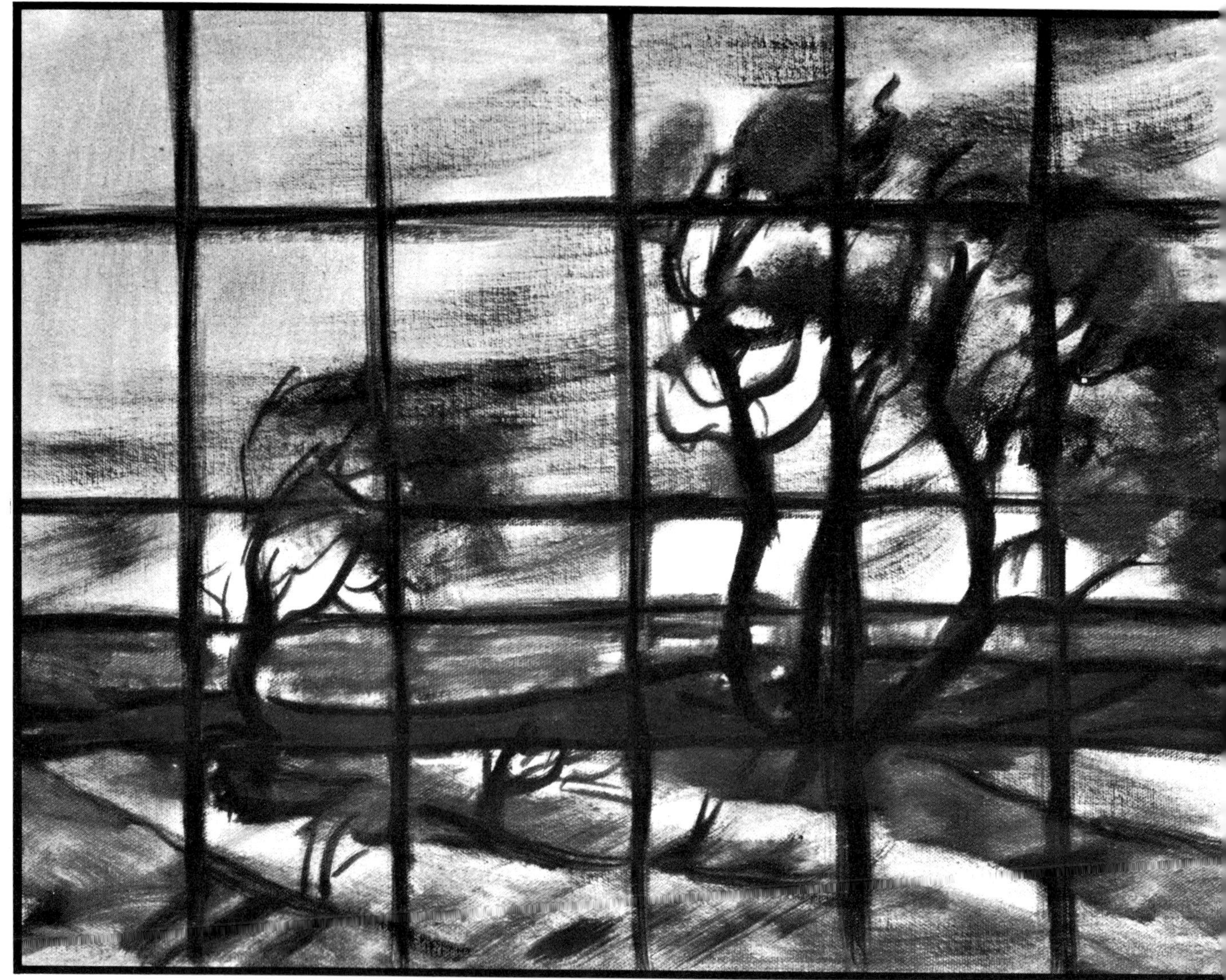

1 Study the foreground in the painting opposite.
2 Paint dark green tone along the coastline in short, uneven strokes.
3 Paint medium and dark green tones on the right side of each rise of ground, using long strokes, and along the bottom and left side of the canvas.
4 Paint dark, medium and light yellow ochre tones on each rise alternately. Use long strokes slanting to the left. Blend tones slightly.
5 Outline the entire edge of the coastline with purple, then add touches of vermilion and aqua here and there.
6 With point of clean knife scratch in tall grasses blowing in the wind, where indicated. Keep them light and delicate.

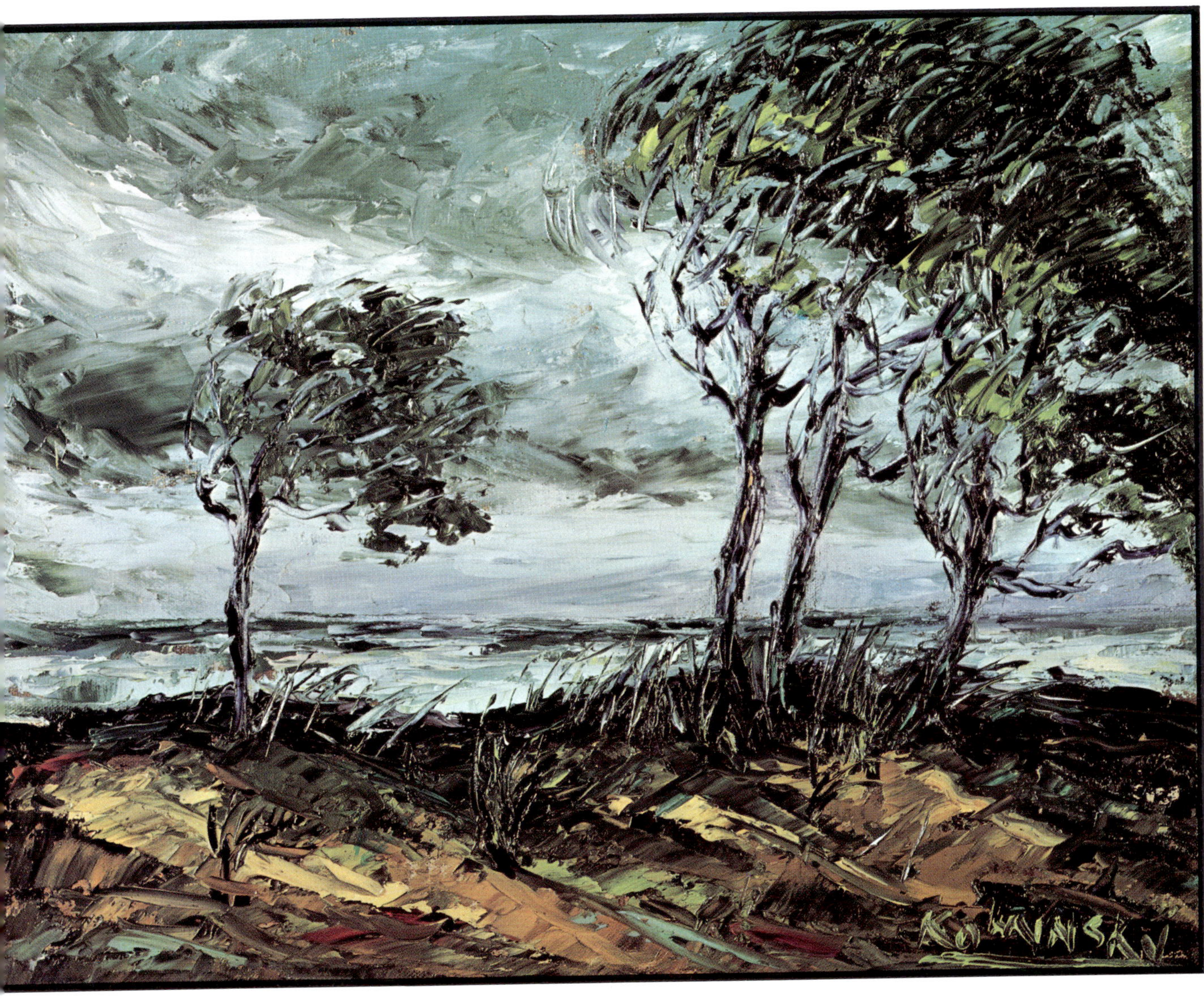

TREES
For best effect the trees should be painted in the wet sky paint.

1 Study the trees in the painting above. Watch the shape and texture.
2 With knife or round brush paint trunks and branches with purple. Paint main branches first, then use knife to scratch in the slender branches. Curve the trunks and branches as indicated.
3 Paint foliage with half-curved strokes of dark green tone going across the branches, to give a wind-blown effect.
4 Paint a few half-curved strokes of medium tone, again going across the branches, then add just a touch of light tone. Do not cover the trees with foliage.
5 With clean knife scratch branches in the foliage.

You will like the dramatic mood in this painting.

Last Three in Totterdown

THE DRAWING

1 Use canvas board, canvas or hardboard, 36cm (14 in.) by 46cm (18 in.) horizontally.
2 Study the drawing and painting on pages 66 and 67.
3 Arrange the palette according to the palette layout on page 8.
4 Use the large, flat hog brush to stain the canvas with a light wash of burnt umber, as described in Step 1 on page 7. Wipe with toilet tissue.
5 With the medium round brush and dark umber wash put in the grid lines and simple drawing as indicated on page 66. For the houses draw a square first on an angle, then add the roof tops and the side of the row of houses, looking up at them.
6 The light is coming from the right, so with dark umber wash lightly shade the front of the houses, the bushes and the area in the centre and right of the canvas.
7 Clean your brushes in the medium of turpentine or white spirit.

THE PAINTING

SKY

**Colour formula
Sky tones**

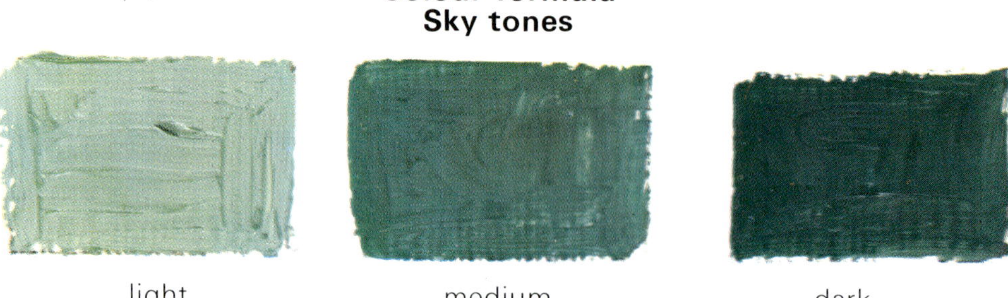

light   medium   dark

Refer to page 26 for sky tones and mix according to the directions.

Let's paint
Use offset knife, held lightly.

1 Study the sky in the painting on page 67.
2 Paint light tone carefully around the houses and along the entire hill.
3 Paint the rest of the sky area with medium tone in long strokes slanting towards the houses. Blend slightly.
4 Paint a little dark tone into the medium tone to give a windswept look.

HOUSES

**Colour formula
Tones of greyed dark green**

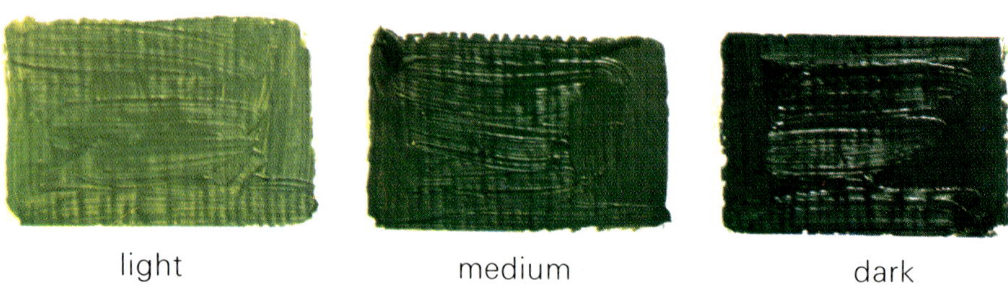

light   medium   dark

Refer to page 36 for tones of greyed dark green and mix according to the directions.

1 Study the houses in the painting on page 67.
2 Paint dark tone on the left of each house, medium tone in the middle and light tone on the right. Blend slightly — the houses should look old and decrepit.
3 Paint the side wall of the righthand house with Naples yellow and add a touch of light greyed dark green tone.
4 Paint a suggestion of windows with purple and add touches of light and medium sky tones where indicated on windows and walls.

ROOFS AND BRICK PILES

Colour tones

to **half the remaining dark greyed dark green tone**
add **¾ teaspoon alizarin crimson**
touch of cadmium orange

to **½ teaspoon light greyed dark green tone**
add **¾ teaspoon vermilion**
touch of cadmium orange

1 Study the roofs and brick piles in the painting on page 67.
2 Paint roofs with dark tone, taking care with the perspective.
3 Paint the large chimney first and then the smaller one with dark and light tones, then paint a suggestion of chimneys on the other roofs in the same way.
4 Outline the roofs and houses lightly with purple.
5 Paint a suggestion of a broken down brick wall in front of the houses with dark and light tones. Do not be precise.
6 Paint a feeling of broken down walls on the upper right of the canvas with medium greyed dark green tone. Add strokes of purple and touches of medium sky tone.
7 Paint the brick pile on the right of the canvas alternately with above dark and light tones. Edge them with purple here and there as indicated.
8 Paint a row of pointed roof tops with chimneys along the top of the hill with purple. Make them very sketchy.

YELLOW GRASSES

Colour formula
Tones of yellow ochre

light   medium   dark

Refer to page 17 for tones of yellow ochre and mix according to the directions.

1 Study the yellow grasses in the painting on page 67.
2 Using the flat of the knife paint light tone across the top of the hill. Stroke the colour across, then downward.
3 Paint alternate medium and dark tones in the yellow grass area, ending up with dark tone at the base of the hill.
4 Paint a few strokes of purple over the dark tone. Keep the whole area textured to

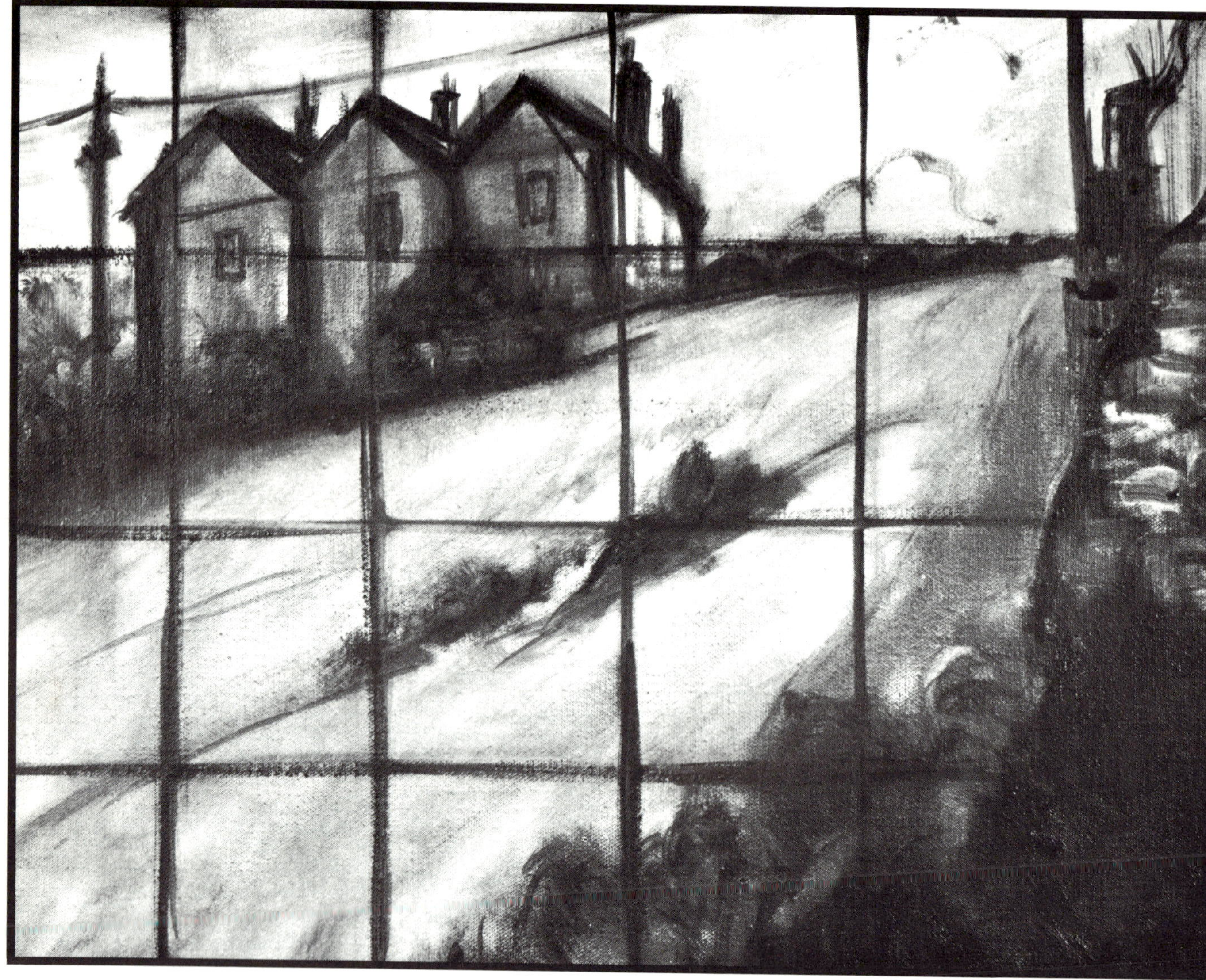

create an impression of long grasses.
5 Paint a few touches of Naples yellow across the light tone, for highlight.

BUSHES

**Colour formula
Tones of green**

light   medium   dark

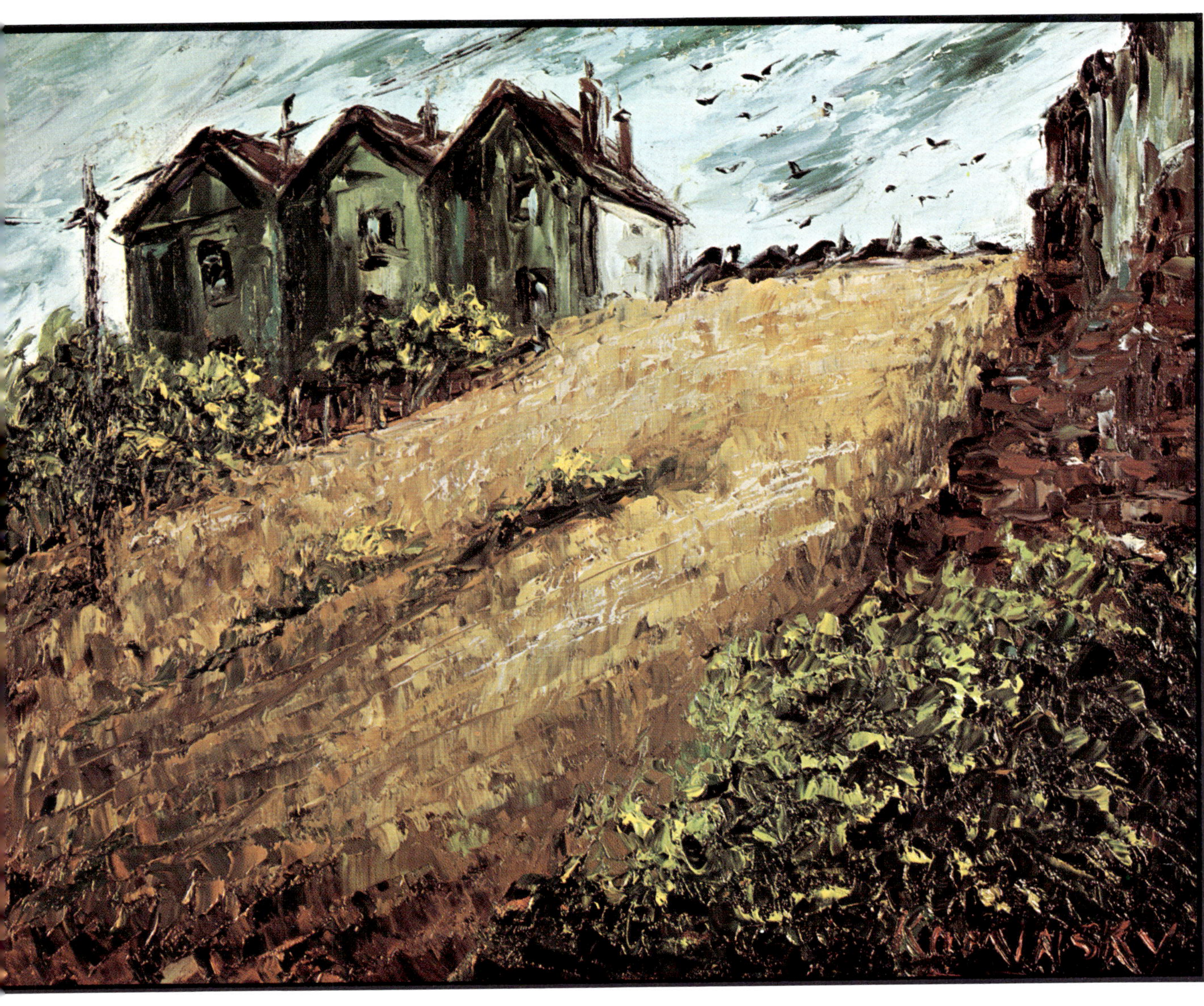

Refer to page 14 for tones of green and mix according to the directions.

1 Study the bushes in the painting above.
2 Paint the bushes on the right of the canvas with short strokes of dark tone. Add touches of purple, then medium and light tones where indicated.
3 Paint bushes in front of the houses by stippling dark tone on the left, medium tone in the middle and light tone on the right of each mass.
4 Paint the little bushes in the yellow grasses and the green grass in the foreground with dark, medium and light tones.
5 Paint the telegraph pole with purple. Keep it slender. Scratch in the telephone wires with the tip of the knife and a little purple.
6 With the tip of the knife and purple carefully paint a flock of small, delicate birds on the right of the houses.

This painting is a good example of eccentric composition — the houses in the upper lefthand corner of the canvas instead of in the centre.

Red Apples

THE DRAWING

1 Use canvas board, canvas or hardboard, 36cm (14 in.) by 46cm (18 in.) vertically.
2 Study the drawing and painting on pages 70 and 71.
3 Arrange the palette according to the palette layout on page 8.
4 Use the large, flat hog brush to stain the canvas with a light wash of burnt umber, as described in Step 1 on page 7. Wipe with toilet tissue.
5 With the medium round brush and dark umber wash put in the grid lines and simple drawing as indicated on page 70. Do not draw in the leaves for now.
6 The light is coming from the left, so with dark umber wash lightly shade in apples where indicated.
7 Clean your brushes in the medium of turpentine or white spirit.

THE PAINTING

BACKGROUND

**Colour formula
Tones of greyed light green**

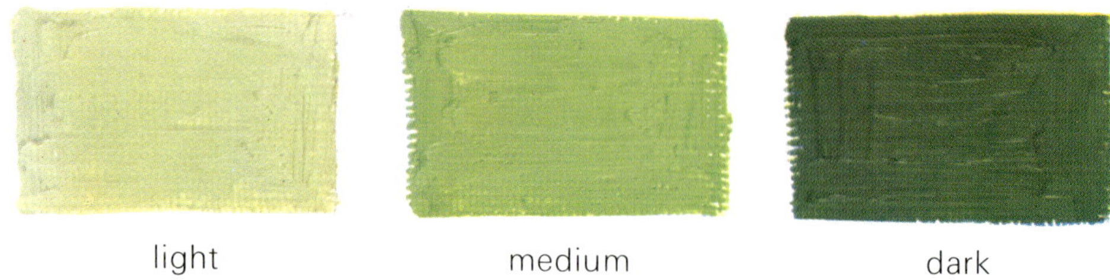

| light | medium | dark |

Refer to page 21 for tones of greyed light green and mix according to the directions.

Let's paint
Use offset knife, held lightly.

1 Study the background in the painting on page 71.
2 Paint dark tone at the top of the canvas to a third of the way down.
3 Paint medium tone in the middle and light tone at the bottom. Blend tones lightly. Go around fruit carefully and if you lose the branches just scratch them back in.

RED APPLES

**Colours
Tones of red**

| cadmium orange | vermilion | alizarin crimson |

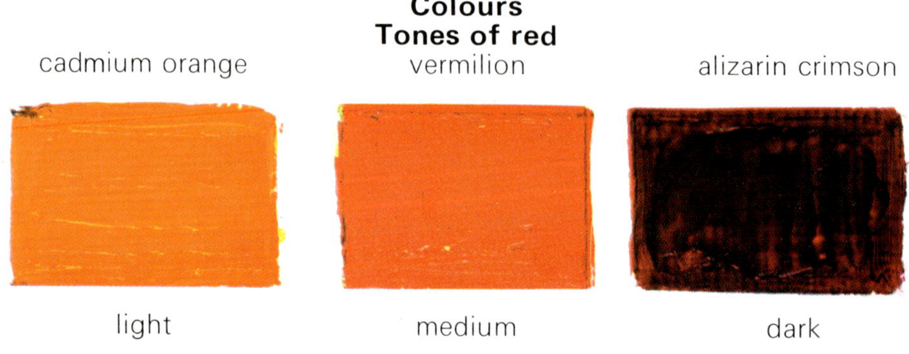

| light | medium | dark |

The tones of red are used from the palette and require no mixing.

1 Study the apples in the painting on page 71.
2 Paint the apple at the top with round strokes of dark tone on the right side, medium tone in the middle and light tone on the left.
3 Paint the two apples in shadow on the extreme right with dark tone. Add a touch of purple to the right side of each and blend lightly.
4 Paint the second apple from the top on the left with dark tone on the right side, medium tone in the middle and light tone on the left side.
5 Paint the centre and left apple in the group of three in the same way. Paint the third apple in the group, in shadow, with dark tone and blend a bit of purple on the right side.
6 Paint the apple on the lower right with dark and medium tones, adding a touch of light tone on the left.
7 Paint the lefthand apple on the bottom branch with dark tone on the right, medium tone in the middle and light tone on the left. Paint the other apple, in shadow, with dark tone, blending in touches of purple.
8 Outline the stem area of each apple with purple painted in a half circle on the left.
9 Paint the other half of this circle with medium tone.

BRANCH
1 Study the branch in the painting on page 71.
2 Paint the entire branch loosely with purple.

LEAVES

**Colour formula
Tones of green**

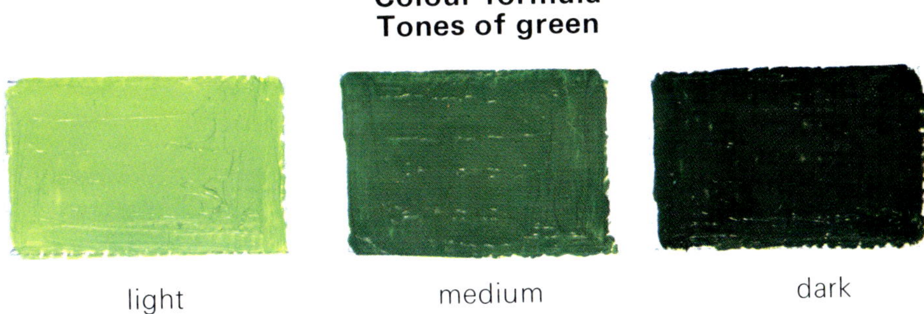

light   medium   dark

Refer to page 14 for tones of green and mix according to the directions.

1 Study the leaves in the painting on page 71.
2 Before applying colour, draw the leaves in with a round brush and purple. This is a slightly different technique.
3 Starting at the top righthand corner paint the leaves with mostly medium and dark tones. Tip some with light tone.
4 Paint the rest of the leaves with dark tone mostly on the right side and medium and light tones on the left side.
5 Use the point of clean knife to outline the leaves, keeping them loose and free.
6 Repaint the branch with purple if you have lost it in painting the leaves.
7 Paint stems of apples with purple and add a highlight of medium green tone.

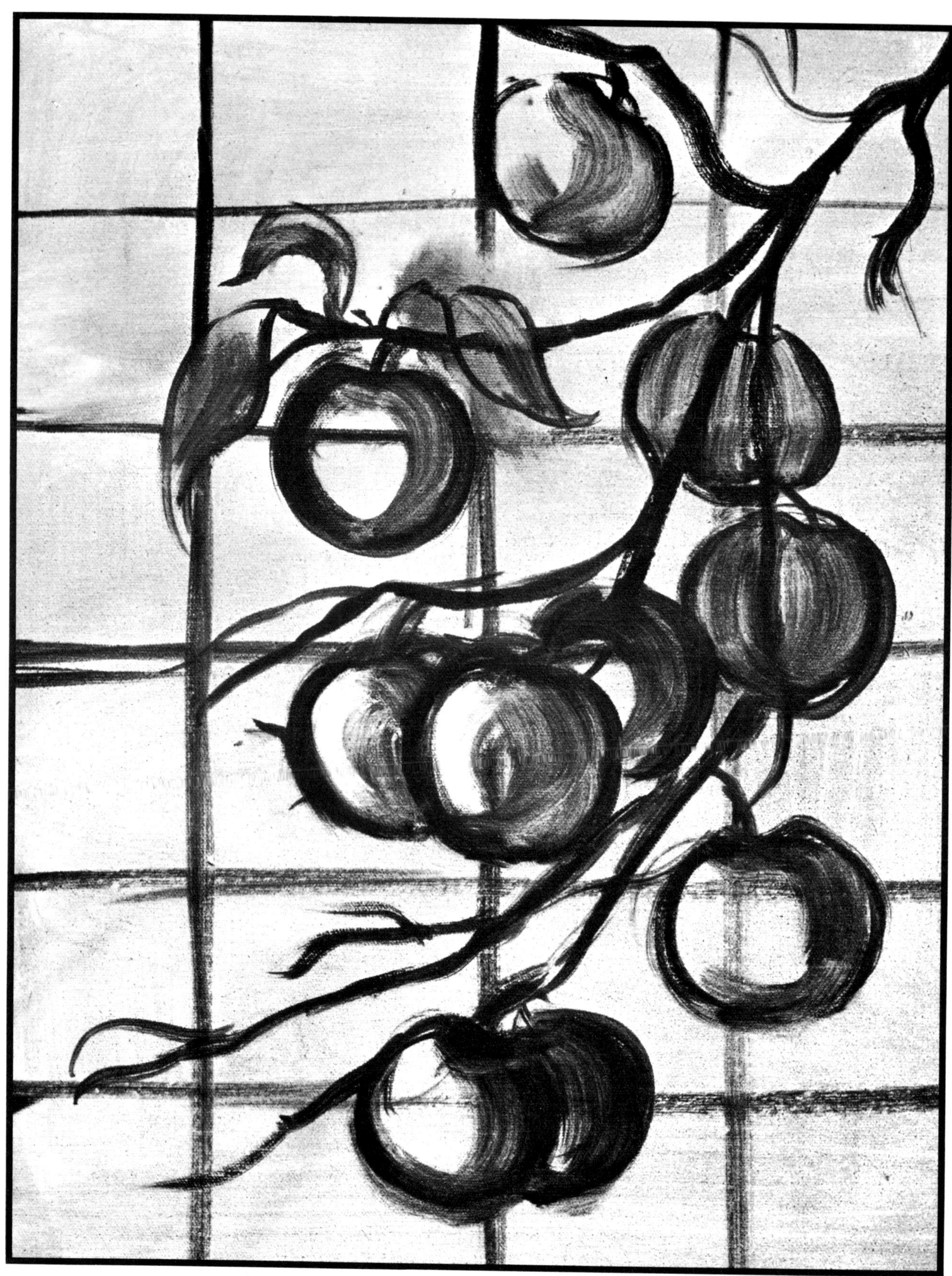

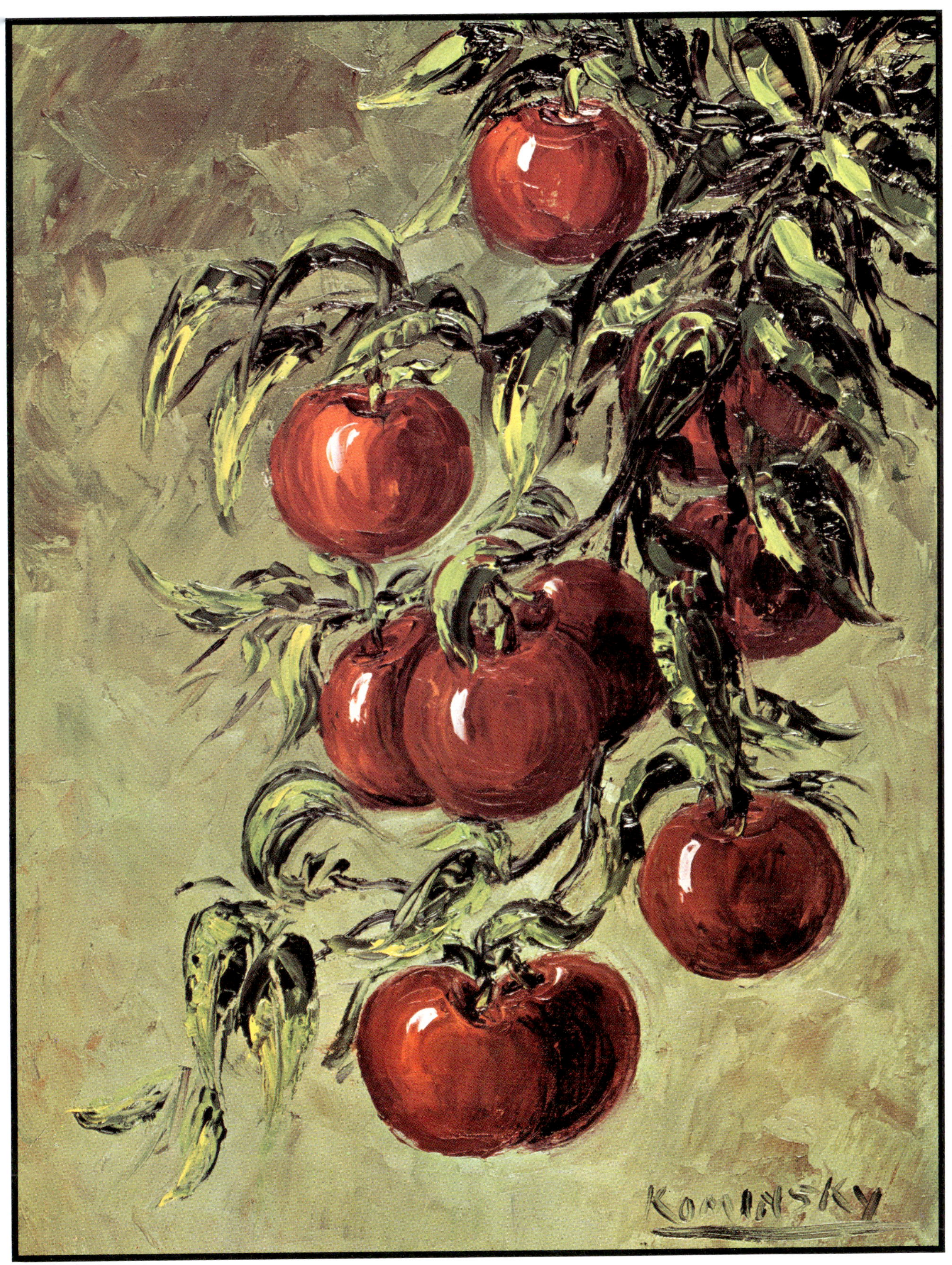

KOMINSKY

HIGHLIGHTS

Colour tone
½ teaspoon white
⅛ teaspoon Naples yellow

1 Study the highlights on the apples in the painting on the previous page.
2 Paint slightly curved strokes of the above tone near the centre of the apples and in the stem area, as indicated.

If someone says, on viewing your apples, 'What lovely tomatoes,' just thank them sweetly — and don't elaborate!

By following the technique outlined in this book, not only will you enjoy learning the basics of painting but you will discover so many fringe benefits. Suddenly you will find you have a greater awareness of the lovely world of colour we live in and a deeper understanding of art and artists. You will find too that you will want to attend art exhibitions, visit all those art galleries you have been promising yourself and maybe attend art classes at the many schools and colleges in the country. Once you enter the world of art, there's no limit to learning.

So keep painting.